Antiques at a Glance

FURNITURE

Antiques at a Glance

FURNITURE

JAMES MACKAY

PRC

Contents

First published 2002 by
PRC Publishing Ltd,
64 Brewery Road, London N7 9NT

A member of **Chrysalis** Books plc

This edition published 2002
Distributed in the U.S. and Canada by:
Sterling Publishing Co., Inc.
387 Park Avenue South
New York, NY 10016

© 2002 PRC Publishing Ltd

ISBN 1 85648 646 X

Printed and bound in China

All the images were kindly supplied by © Christie's
Images Ltd 2002.

Introduction

Humanity is perhaps not unique in the habit of storing up objects for their own sake, but is the only animal capable of translating material possessions into other values and assessing their worth in terms of hard cash.

According to the Encyclopaedia Britannica "antique" means "old" but also carries connotations of esthetic, historic, or financial value. Formerly the term was applied to the remains of the classical cultures of Greece and Rome, now more specifically labeled as "antiquities," but gradually "decorative arts, courtly, bourgeois, and peasant, of all past eras came to be considered antique."

This definition is somewhat vague, though it hints that mere age alone is not sufficient to make an object worthy of the appellation "antique." The *Oxford English Dictionary* is even more vague in its definition: "Having existed since olden times; of a good age, venerable, old-fashioned, antiquated such as is no longer extant; out of date, behind the times, stale; of, belonging to, or after the manner of any ancient time; a relic of ancient art, of bygone days."

The legal definition of an antique also varied considerably from one country to another. The United Kingdom Customs and Excise Tariff law of 1930 specified that objects manufactured before 1830 (i.e. a hundred years old or more) would be regarded as antique and therefore exempt from payment of duty on import. The United States Tariff Act of 1930 exempted from duty "Artistic antiquities, collections in illustration of the progress of the arts, objects of art of educational value or ornamental character...which shall have been produced prior to the year 1830." Across the border in Canada, however, the Customs Tariff Act of 1948 defined as antiquities "all objects of educational value and museum interest, if produced prior to 1st January 1847."

Thus legal definitions, originally designed to cover material a century old, became fixed in such a way as to exclude anything produced after the Regency period. It was often stated that the main reason for adhering to the year 1830 was the fact that craftsmanship deteriorated after that date. For this reason bodies, such as the British Antique Dealers' Association, clung to 1830 as the chronological criterion in defining an antique.

As time passed, however, this inflexible ruling seemed more and more untenable from a purely legal viewpoint, and for the purpose of the avoidance of the payment of import duty the date criterion was subsequently modified in certain countries. The United Kingdom Customs and Excise Tariff Act of 1959, for example, outlined that duty would not be payable on the import of objects "if manufactured or produced as a whole, and in the form as imported, more than a hundred years before the date of import." More recently, the United States customs adopted a straightforward hundred-year rule, and with the advent of Value Added Tax and similar imposts in other countries, the hundred-year rule is now widely observed.

In periods of economic uncertainty interest in collectable objects tends to increase at the expense of more traditional forms of investment. What used to be the principal motive in collecting—a need to identify with the past—has tended to yield to a need for the form of security that the possession of tangible objects brings when money itself is diminishing in worth and true meaning. It becomes less important to the collector to amass objects of great antiquity, especially since the supply of antiques has become scarcer due to worldwide demand, and leads the collector to turn inevitably to more recent products. For those reasons, therefore, many dealers in the 1970s and 1980s adopted a fifty-year rule, so that objects of the 1920s

Left: A German walnut and oak cabinet-on-stand, circa 1900.

their collections. This meant that the amount of quality antiques available to the market began to dry up, as well as having the unfortunate effect of pushing up the market value of what material was left. Some categories of antiques, such as 16th and 17th-century silver, early Meissen and Chelsea porcelain, and Ravenscroft glass, soon went beyond the reach of all but the wealthiest collectors. Not only did museums tend to create a shortage of material available to the private collector but, by imaginative and intelligent use of their acquisitions, they heightened the interest of established collectors and laymen alike, thereby increasing the demand for antiques still further.

While this tendency was gathering momentum in the 1960s and 1970s, the growing interest in the private sector was inevitable anyway. A higher level of general prosperity and higher standards of education were only two of the factors which made the public not only more appreciative of all that was best from times past, but also gave them the money to indulge their tastes. Traditionally antique collecting had been the closed preserve of the upper classes, who had the money, the education, and the social background to indulge their tastes. Collecting antiquities developed in Renaissance Italy and spread slowly to more northerly countries. In Britain, for example, the fashion for collecting things of the past only really began to develop in the late 18th century. Emphasis was laid on classical antiquities, fostered by the classical education of the times as well as the acquisitive habits picked up during the obligatory Grand Tour.

From then on, an antiquarian interest in the material objects of the past tended to lag behind by one or two centuries. Thus collectors of the Regency era discovered an interest in Tudor and Jacobean furniture, the Victorians looked to the Restoration and early Georgian period, and

and 1930s could be encompassed. First the artifacts of the late Victorian and Art Nouveau periods became perfectly acceptable, and were then rapidly followed by Art Deco and the products of the immediate prewar period. Now date lines have been virtually abandoned as collectors and dealers discover newer and newer objects on which to focus their attention.

Greater flexibility in defining what might be regarded as an antique came not a moment too soon, as the supply of fine-quality pieces produced before 1830 had all but dried up by the 1960s. At the same time, many museums with seemingly unlimited funds were intent on expanding the Edwardians had the highest regard for the products of the 18th and early 19th centuries. In general collectors and cognoscente alike disregarded the products of their immediate forebears, which explains why the 1830 rule endured as long as it did.

Interest in collectables has also gone in cycles. There are five or ten-year highs and lows in different categories, as well as periods of slump due to socio-political and economic factors. Antiques that came on to the market in 1917 or 1942, for example, could be picked up for a song. However, people didn't have the money to spend in those years, and there was a general reluctance to invest in material that might be destroyed by enemy action or plundered in the uncertainties of war.

Conversely, the economic upheavals of the late 1960s and early 1970s led to a flight of money out of traditional forms of investment, such as stocks, shares, unit trusts, real estate, and building societies, and into art and antiques. The devaluation of sterling in November 1967 and the subsequent run on the dollar and then the franc created a wave of near hysteria in the antique markets of Europe and America. The leading salesrooms reported a 50 percent increase in turnover in the ensuing 12 months alone, right across the board, although in certain categories the turnover was up by as much as 100 percent (for prints and drawings), while silver sales increased by 69 percent.

Coupled with this astonishing increase in sales, it was significant that the leading salesrooms on both sides of the Atlantic began diversifying into material of more recent vintage than was generally accepted as antique, and this trend has steadily developed ever since. This even led to the development of separate auction houses, such as Christie's in South Kensington, London, catering specifically to the "newer" antiques, including many articles that would not have been regarded as collectable a few years previously.

The major salesrooms, as well as the multitudes of lesser auction houses, were only encouraging a trend that was already there. In the same way, the junk shop of yesteryear has been elevated to the antique shop of today; the weekend junk stall or barrow in a street market has become a booth in a permanent antique market; and the better pieces traded in market sales rapidly move up the scale, with a corresponding mark-up in price at each stage.

As the amount of quality antiques available to the market dwindled, it seemed paradoxical that antique shops were proliferating everywhere at an astonishing rate. The number of good antique shops remained fairly static, nor did they find it any easier to obtain quality material for their stock. The answer to this paradox was, at first, a general lowering of standards; if you clung to increasingly untenable date lines, whether 1830 or 1870, then it was inevitable that you had to settle for second-best or some sacrifice in workmanship, condition, or quality.

The more astute collectors ignored date lines and explored the potential of later material. If the products of the Baroque, Rococo, and Neoclassical periods were no longer available, might not there be much to commend in, say, the products of the Second Empire in France, the Biedermeier era in Germany, or the Victorian era in general? It was fashionable at one time to write off the entire Victorian period as one of uniformly bad taste. Much of the opprobrium heaped on the bourgeois fashions of the 19th century by subsequent generations was undeserved. It is true that in furniture and art, as in the material comforts of everyday life, the Victorians showed a predilection for the massive, the ornate, and the fussy; but not all was tawdry or tasteless by any means.

That the Victorians were capable of perpetrating, and apparently enjoying, objects of unbelievable hideousness is true, but at the same time there were serious attempts to raise standards. The much-abused Great Exhibition of 1851 did more than is often realized to encourage pride in craftsmanship and demonstrate that a thing could be beautiful as well as functional. Though much that is Victorian was, not so long ago, regarded as hardly worth preserving, there were many other things that possessed

Above: A German ormolu-mounted walnut canape circa 1900.

enduring qualities, and were recognized as such by discerning collectors, long before such objects had earned the title or dignity of antique. It has to be added that even the fussy and the florid, the over-ornamented, and the downright ugly from that much-maligned period have acquired a certain period charm. Truly, distance does lend enchantment.

Conscious efforts to improve public taste and foster pride in workmanship seem like oases in the wilderness of materialism and mass production. In England, the Arts and Crafts Movement inspired by William Morris in the 1880s was an attempt to recapture something of the primeval simplicity in craftsmanship—a reaction against the pomposity and over-ornateness of Victorian taste. It was a precursor of that curious phenomenon at the turn of the century known as Art Nouveau in Britain, as Jugendstil ("youth style") in Germany, or as Liberty style in Italy (from the well-known London department store which was one of its great proponents). The practitioners of the New Art went back to nature for inspiration, and invested their furniture, glass, silver, and ceramics with sinuous lines and an ethereal quality. In turn, this provoked a reaction which resulted in the straight lines of the Bauhaus and the geometric forms associated with Art Deco in the interwar period.

It has to be admitted that these styles and fashions seemed ludicrous to many people at the time, especially in their more exaggerated forms; nevertheless they were the outward expression of a minority in art, in architecture, in furniture, textile, and ceramic design, which strove for improvements (as they saw it) in the production and appearance of objects. These were not only objects intended purely for decorative purposes, but those used in every phase and aspect of life.

The products of the Arts and Crafts Movement, Art Nouveau, and Art Deco were despised and neglected in succession, and then, after a decent lapse of time, people began to see them in their proper perspective and appreciate that they had a great deal to offer to the collector.

Nevertheless, it is also fair to comment that the century after 1830 was a barren one as far as the production of fine-quality material was concerned. Thirty years ago collectors made a fine distinction between what was merely old but had no particular merit on grounds of esthetic features or workmanship, and those objects which had some qualities to commend them. Nowadays, however, as demand continues to outstrip supply, there is a tendency to talk up wares that may be old, but are commonplace and mediocre nonetheless. The insatiable demand especially at the lowest end of the market decrees that this should be so, but it is important for the collector to discriminate and learn to recognize the features and factors that distinguish the worthwhile from the second-rate. Ultimately these are the factors that govern the soundness of any investment in antiques.

In the course of this century there have been startling developments in education, communications, travel, and living standards. Today, people are generally more affluent than were their parents or grandparents. They enjoy shorter working hours and a larger surplus disposable income. Through education and such external stimuli as the cinema and television, they have a greater awareness of things of beauty or antiquarian interest. More and more people now have the time and the money to indulge in what was formerly the preserve of a privileged few.

A greater general awareness of what is beautiful and worthwhile inevitably tends to encourage better craftsmanship. Despite the general perception of the period between the two world wars as the nadir in fine design and workmanship there were also many individuals and groups who were active in Europe and America in promoting design consciousness. Today, the products of their studios and workshops, especially in the fields of furniture, ceramics, glass, and metalwork, are deservedly sought after and fetch correspondingly high prices. This trend has continued right down to the present day, with the result that each year the artifacts created by the most imaginative and innovative graduates of the art schools and colleges are eagerly snapped up as the antiques of the future.

Britain, which led the way in the mid 19th century, also pioneered attempts to foster good design in an infinite range of useful articles, from household appliances to postage stamps, through the medium of the government-sponsored Design Centre and the Council of Industrial Design. During World War II, when there was a shortage of materials and manpower, these schemes helped to develop the utility concept, which extended over the entire range of manufactured goods. At the time, "utility" was often equated with shoddy and second-rate, but in more recent times collectors have begun to appreciate the simple lines of the applied arts of the so-called austerity period.

There was a time when objects were collected for their own sakes; as examples of exquisite craftsmanship, beauty, or rarity. Perhaps the reason for collecting was nothing more than the charm of owning something of great age. At any rate, intrinsic worth was seldom of primary consideration. Nowadays, however, there is a tendency for the collector to be aware of values and to prize his possessions not only for their esthetic qualities, but also as investments.

Gone are the days of the great gentleman-collectors, such as Sloane, Cotton, Harley, Hunter, Hearst, and Burrell, whose interests covered every collectable medium and whose tastes were equally developed for paintings and incunabula as for coins and illuminated manuscripts. Even the computer billionaires of the present day could scarcely emulate the feat of the late Andrew Mellon, who in the 1920s once purchased 33 paintings from the Hermitage for $19 million. But while there are very few private individuals, who could now afford to buy a Leonardo, a Rembrandt, or even a Van Gogh, there are millions of people throughout the world who have the leisure to specialize in some chosen field, and the surplus cash to acquire the material for their collections. There are countless afficionados who have formed outstanding collections of porcelain, silver, prints, or glass, who have specialized in the products of individual potteries, or Depression glass, or Kilner paperweights, or Goss china. At the lower end of the spectrum there are hundreds of different classes of collectable, from the frankly ludicrous, such as bricks, barbed wire, and lavatory chain-pulls, to the fetishistic, including whips and certain articles of ladies' apparel. There are also collectors of commemorative wares and even objects associated with one's profession, such as dental and medical instruments. The collecting virus is now endemic and insatiable.

Styles and Periods
For all practical purposes collectable antiques date from the late 15th and 16th centuries. Furniture from this period tends to be massive and made of oak or indigenous timbers such as elm and yew. Chests, stools, small tables, paneled chairs, sideboards, aumbries, wall-cupboards, and refectory tables form the bulk of the furniture. Much of what is described generically as treen comes into this category: wooden trenchers and platters, turned wooden bowls, and bread-boards. Cutlery consists largely of bone-handled knives and horn spoons, though horn continued to be used in rural areas well into the 18th century. Pewter dishes, flagons, and tankards are still available, as are broad-bowled pewter spoons. The equivalent in silver, with relatively plain shanks and a flat end, are now elusive and very expensive. Late-medieval glass, mainly imported from Venice, is rare in fine condition.

Maiolica pottery, in the form of drug jars, dishes, jugs, and flagons, with polychrome decoration, was produced in Urbino, Faenza, and other Italian towns and exported to northern and western Europe. Here again, good quality maiolica is scarce and worth a king's ransom when it passes through the salesroom. Textile materials include embroidery panels, caps and coifs, gloves, purses, and decorated caskets. Not long ago such material could still be

Above: A pair of mahogany lowboys in George II style with elements of the 18th century .

picked up for reasonable sums but, like everything else from this early period, prices have now gone through the roof.

In the Elizabethan and Jacobean period (approximately 1560–1660) the dominant feature is furniture. Politically and economically, what the Tudors had struggled to accomplish was consolidated in the first half of the 17th century. Although the civil wars and the aftermath of the Commonwealth tend to give the impression of disorder, it was, by and large, a period of rising prosperity and it was

the emergence of the wealthy middle classes which precipitated the power struggle with the monarchy.

The styles initiated in furniture during the latter part of the Tudor period were gradually developed during the reigns of the first Stuart kings. It is rather in the expansion of the market that the furniture known as Jacobean stands out from its predecessors. Whereas chairs and tables were hitherto relatively uncommon, a great variety of these objects were developed in the time of James I (1603–25) and Charles I (1625–49). In many respects, Jacobean furniture had the same hallmarks as its Tudor counterparts, but these characteristics were accentuated and carried to their logical conclusion, while the wider variety of objects and the greater quantity manufactured have popularized the label "Jacobean" applied to much of the furniture produced in Britain in the 17th century.

Apart from stools, the Elizabethan household would have boasted few chairs, and many of these would, in effect, have consisted of chests adapted for sitting on. Box seats continued to be fashionable under the Stuarts but were given various refinements such as arms and paneled backs. Gradually the box element was phased out and an open frame adopted, the legs being kept rigid by means of massive stretchers. Joined box-chairs (the Coronation chair in Westminster Abbey is a fine example) had existed since the 14th century, but were confined to the households of the nobility and the wealthiest classes. They only became popular with the poorest classes toward the end of the 16th century and were almost entirely superseded in the Jacobean period by chairs on the open-frame pattern.

Joined furniture developed slowly in the early 1600s. Indigenous timbers, mainly oak, elm, and yew, were used extensively in the production of solid, utilitarian pieces which were evidently built to last. Because of the robust nature of its design a very large proportion of Jacobean furniture has survived to the present day. Curiously enough, a great deal of lighter, upholstered furniture was also manufactured in the same period but this, owing to the perishable nature of the materials involved, has not survived in the same quantity. Chairs and stools of this sort were generally constructed in beech, a type of wood which is particularly prone to attack from furniture beetles and other wood-boring insects. The fabric and stuffing employed did not stand up to hard usage and it is significant that the few extant examples (mostly in museum collections) present a sadly dilapidated appearance.

Furniture produced during the Commonwealth period tended to be more austere and devoid of frivolity. Fine satin fabrics, and even the harder wearing "Turkey" work (so-called because it resembled the Turkish carpets which were beginning to be popular in western Europe at that time) were frowned upon, and the manufacturers substituted leather upholstery secured by large brass-headed nails. After the Restoration of 1660, traditional styles continued, but with an increasing amount of decoration. Elaborate punch-work was used on high-paneled backs, often incorporating the date or initials of the owner. Effective use was made of turnery not only in the legs and stretchers but in the smaller supports to the arms of chairs.

In ceramics, Italian maiolica vied with early French faience, but by the end of the 16th century Delft in Holland was an important center for tin-glazed earthenware, mainly blue and white in decoration in imitation of the Oriental porcelains which were now beginning to be imported through the East India Company and its European rivals. In the early 17th century delftware became a generic term for decorative earthenware manufactured at London, Liverpool, Bristol, and Wincanton in England as well as at Dublin, Limerick, and the aptly named Delftfield in Glasgow, each area producing its own distinctive variation. The blue-dash chargers of the late 17th and early 18th centuries are much sought after, not only on aesthetic grounds but also for their historic significance, being often decorated with portraits of royalty. Mugs, beakers, barbers' basins, bleeding bowls, and apothecaries' jars as well as rack-plates provide ample scope for the collector. Much of this material belongs to a later period, delftware remaining fashionable till the late 18th century.

Soda glass continued to be imported mainly from Venice throughout the Jacobean period and examples in fine condition are now very expensive. The Venetian monopoly was broken by George Ravenscroft who experimented with christalline glass in the Restoration period and by 1675 had evolved an entirely new type of glass containing lead oxide. The lead content was gradually increased and by the beginning of the 18th century had taken on its heavy, dark, brilliant appearance.

In Britain, silver dating before the Restoration is very rare, largely as a result of the Civil War period when much of the existing plate was melted down and converted into coin to pay the troops on opposing sides. Small articles, notably spoons, have survived from the Jacobean period but are now very highly priced, especially those decorated with figures of the apostles.

In the Restoration period, which extended to the end of the 17th century and beyond, there was a return to the more florid styles of decoration in furniture, a reaction to the austerely simple lines favored during the Puritan Commonwealth. It should be noted that American colonial furniture of this period tended to retain the simpler lines, influenced by the styles imported by the Pilgrim Fathers in 1620, and this penchant for clean lines and a minimum of decoration continued right through to the Shaker furniture of the 19th century and even the forms developed in the early part of this century.

Styles in Britain as the 17th century drew to a close were strongly influenced by the Baroque fashions which originated in Italy and spread to Spain, France, and Germany, and which were largely introduced to England by the influx of Huguenot refugees after the revocation of the Edict of Nantes in 1685 increased the persecution of non-Catholics. Baroque (literally the French word for "irregular") was characterized by asymmetrical, curving lines but gradually developed into extravagant and elaborate ornament, festooned with ribbons, scrolls, swags, shells, cornucopias, and cupids. Furniture was not only carved but often overlaid with gilt gesso work. It was now much lighter in construction, but the craze for curving lines extended to legs and chairbacks. Similar excrescences decorated pottery, glass, and silver.

This period also witnessed the growth of walnut in popularity. Walnut trees had been grown in England since Tudor times but it was not till after the Restoration that it came into fashion as a furniture timber. Even then, the coarse texture of English walnut and its comparative lack of figuring made it less popular than French, Italian, and Spanish walnut, and latterly the black American variety. The heyday of walnut in English furniture came in the period from 1660–1720, though it remained fairly fashionable

as late as the 1760s. The most desirable pieces of walnut furniture now in existence emanate from the later Stuart period during which craftsmen acquired Continental techniques of cabinetmaking and produced much elegant furniture with a certain flamboyance characteristic of the Restoration era.

Tremendous impetus to the development of more delicate styles in furniture came in the 1690s; to this period belong the graceful cabinets, chests of drawers, and bookcases which attained their best phase in the reign of Queen Anne (1702–14). When combined with marquetry veneer panels and crossbanding in contrasting timbers such as rosewood and sycamore, walnut produced highly pleasing decorative effects.

In 1664 the Worshipful Company of Glass-sellers and Looking-glass Manufacturers was incorporated and in the same year George Villiers, second Duke of Buckingham, obtained a patent to make glass. He established a factory at Vauxhall, London, and by the end of the 17th century the production of mirrors had expanded enormously. They continued to be relatively expensive and it was not until about 1740 that they became at all plentiful. Thereafter they became increasingly popular, especially when extravagantly decorated in the Rococo style.

During the same period English pottery began to compete successfully with imported wares although there was nothing to equal the hard-paste porcelain which flooded in from China. The blue and white motifs on Chinese ceramics triggered off a craze for chinoiserie which influenced other forms of the applied arts, from furniture to textiles and metalwork. Certain Oriental decorative arts made a tremendous impact; the fashion for ivory and jade dates from the beginning of the 18th century. Lacquered furniture was introduced to western Europe from the Far East in the latter part of the 16th century, but the wares imported from China and Japan by the Portuguese were relatively minor pieces, mainly chests and small cabinets. Nevertheless the dark glossy appearance of these items was a refreshing change to the dull, massy furniture which graced the homes of the wealthy classes and it was not long before lacquerware was being imitated in the Low Countries and England.

Oriental lacquer was based on ground varnishes of various colors with lengthy drying periods between many coats which might take up to three years to reach perfection. Western imitators were hampered by lack of the proper materials but by the middle of the 17th century had succeeded in manufacturing a tolerable substitute. Inevitably japanning, as the European technique was known, failed to achieve the brilliant lustre and durability which characterized Oriental lacquer. The japanning of furniture, however, received great stimulus in 1688 when John Stalker and George Parker published their treatise on japanning and varnishing. In the period from 1690–1730 japanned furniture decorated with chinoiserie was all the rage. Thereafter, it declined in fashion and was virtually eclipsed by 1750, until 1780 when it revived again for a short time and was also briefly in favor in the early 1800s.

Britain emerged as a world power in the early 18th century, after the brilliant successes of its forces in the War of the Spanish Succession. In later conflicts Britain rivaled France for the mastery of the colonial world, in India and the Western Hemisphere and emerged triumphant in 1763. The accession of the Hanoverian kings in 1714 increasingly involved Britain in European politics and artistic influences. Despite the Jacobite rebellions of 1715 and 1745, Britain enjoyed a long period of relative stability and rising prosperity. Greater affluence was reflected in the furniture, silverware, and decorative arts of the period.

The Georgian era is conveniently divided into Early Georgian, covering the reigns of the first two Georges (1714–60), and Late Georgian, corresponding with the long reign of George III (1760–1820). The era as a whole witnessed a tremendous development in architecture which, in turn, influenced styles in the applied and decorative arts. The Early Georgian period coincided with the

zenith of the Baroque in Europe, with its emphasis on curves and scrolls in everything from the legs of tables to the handles of coffee pots. Scallops and acanthus leaves decorated the corners and joints of furniture as well as the rims of vessels.

The craze for curved lines culminated in the 1730s with the rise of rococo, a much lighter, more delicate style than Baroque and clearly a reaction against its tendency to the massive and fussy. The Italianate word was actually derived from two French terms—*rocaille* (rockwork) and *coquille* (shell). It arose out of the vogue for grottoes in landscape gardening and was characterized by floral swags and garlands, as well as C and S curves in great profusion. Britain lagged behind the Continent so it was not until the middle of the century that the Rococo fashion reached its height in England. It lent itself very well to setting off Oriental motifs, later joined by Indian art forms and continued, in a more restrained form, right through to the end of the 18th century. In general Rococo represented a much lighter approach to form and decoration than the baroque. By the end of the century, however, styles were becoming more eclectic, often blending the Rococo with the neoclassical and even the gothic, an artificial revival of certain medieval forms such as pointed arches.

In this period, mahogany and other hardwoods from the Caribbean gradually supplanted walnut as the preferred medium for furniture. Newer shapes and styles included the *bombé* chest of drawers and the glass-fronted bookcase with broken pediment top. The dominant personality in furniture design in this period was William Kent (1685–1748), the first English architect to include furniture design as an integral part of his interior decoration. On chairs and tables, the technique of "hipping" the legs to the seat or table-top encouraged the ornamentation of the joint. Several motifs were used, among them the cabochon and leaf ornament and the lion, satyr, or human mask being the most popular. The comparative lack of figuring in mahogany was compensated for by the addition of a certain amount of carving, fretting, and piercing, made possible by the greater strength of West Indian hardwoods. This was the great period of the table in all its various forms and the dining table first became widely popular at this time. Smaller, lighter forms, from the folding games table to the small sewing table, were also developed in this period and remain immensely popular to this day.

In glassware this was the period of much lighter forms, encouraged by the Glass Excise Act of 1745 which taxed glass by weight. The massive drinking glasses fashionable in the period from 1685–1720 gave way to the more elegant baluster glasses with knopped stems as the century progressed, and by 1750 became much lighter, the deliberate use of air bubbles (which had originally occurred by accident) leading to air twist stems of amazing intricacy.

Meissen and Sèvres pioneered European porcelain in the first half of the century but it was not until 1750 that the manufacture of similar wares began at Derby, followed by Worcester (from 1751), Chelsea (1745–69), and Bow (1746–76). English bone china rivaled the French and German products in its uniformly high quality in composition, decoration, and potting. There was, of course, a penchant for Chinese and Japanese decoration but European flowers, penciled motifs, armorial features, and transfer-printed ornament were also popular. The shapes favored by the potters were closely modeled on the Rococo styles used by contemporary silversmiths, but there was an enormous demand for figurines, groups, and centerpieces.

The Early Georgian period was the heyday of the great Huguenot silversmith, Paul de Lamerie who embarked on his career in 1712. The early work produced by him is relatively austere in design, the simple forms relieved only by engraving or applied strapwork, fine flat-chasing, and the masks and scrolls so dear to French craftsmen of the late 17th century. As the 18th century progressed, the style of de Lamerie's work was modified considerably and this influenced his contemporaries. During the 1720s, there

was a tendency toward greater elaboration, both in shapes and ornament, which found formal expression in the Rococo styles of the following decade. Rococo silver reached its zenith in the decade before de Lamerie's death in 1751 and, as the prime exponent of the style in silver, he was perhaps rather too fond of the massive decoration which characterizes it. Nevertheless his work, with few exceptions, outclassed that of his contemporaries and the discernment of collectors right down to the present ensures that his products fetch very large sums when they turn up in the salesroom.

Devotees of fine English furniture are almost unanimous in the view that the latter half of the 18th century and the opening decades of the 19th marked the zenith of English cabinetmaking. The Late Georgian period witnessed the happy combination of brilliance in design with the perfection in production techniques developed over the centuries, and a wide range of excellent materials never before available in such quantities.

Thomas Chippendale's celebrated *Director*, published in 1754, was only one of the numerous manuals which greatly stimulated good furniture design. Batty and Langley produced their *Treasury of Designs* under the baroque influence of Kent, whereas the *New Book of Ornaments* by Matthias Lock in 1752 favored the Rococo style, and chinoiserie and "gothick" styles found expression in the writings of Matthias Darly and the Halfpennys, William and his son John, in the same period.

The techniques in the manufacture of furniture reached their peak in the same period. Vast improvements in the industry had been made possible by the tremendous growth of the market for good quality pieces which enabled cabinetmakers to expand their businesses and turn over whole sections of their factories to specialisation.

Hitherto, the bulk of the best work was concentrated in the London area, but now the provincial cabinetmakers were emerging as manufacturers of furniture no longer content to ape the fashions of the metropolis (often decades behind) but were producing excellent pieces in

Above: A French ormolu-mounted, kingwood breakfront library cabinet, late 19th century.

the latest fashions and even, as in the case of craftsmen such as Richard Gillow of Lancaster, originating furniture designs for the Londoners to follow. It should not be overlooked either that Thomas Chippendale himself was a Yorkshireman, born at Otley in 1718. After completing his apprenticeship he moved to London and established his workshop there in 1749. Although he dominated English furniture design throughout the second half of the 18th century, other cabinetmakers whose work has been the subject of reappraisal in recent years include his great rivals William Vile and John Cobb, while William Hallett, John Channon, and Pierre Langlois were not far behind. Chippendale and his imitators were at their best when blending the Rococo of Louis Quinze with chinoiserie and the gothic of Walpole's Strawberry Hill. As well as developing the cabriole leg, they introduced the Chinese claw and ball foot, the straight, angular lines of mid-Georgian, the "Gothick" fretwork leg, and the Chinese lattice back.

In ceramics English craftsmen were also making enormous strides and creating distinctive innovations. This was the era of Josiah Wedgwood, pioneer of Queen's Ware for teasets and other tablewares. Later he turned his attention to various forms of stoneware, first black basaltes, and jasperware in which white cameos and reliefs were set against a ground of pale pastel colors. Both materials were utilized in the production of a huge range of useful and ornamental pottery which laid the foundations of timeless classical lines that remain popular to this day. Many potteries sprang up in this period, competing with each other in the fields of earthenware and soft-paste porcelain. Today, the products of Coalport and Caughley, Lowestoft and Longton Hall, Leeds, New Hall, Rockingham, Spode, Swansea, and Minton have their devotees.

One medium which went through a rather lean time in this period was silver. As a result of its interminable Continental wars, Britain was habitually cut off from the normal sources of supply, and even coinage in this metal was often in short supply. Much of the silver that survives from this period consists of small articles, such as shoe-

buckles, wine labels, and decorative objects like vinaigrettes and snuff boxes. Wine labels and other small items below 10 dwt in weight were exempt from hallmarking under the Plate Offence Act of 1738 and were therefore marked only on a voluntary and sporadic basis. The Marking Silver Plate Act of 1790, however, stipulated that silver bottle-tickets, whatever their weight, had to be hallmarked. From then onward silver wine labels present little problem either in dating or in the correct ascription of their manufacturer.

The need for hollowwares that bore a passing resemblance at least to silver induced industrial entrepreneurs like Matthew Boulton of Soho, Birmingham, to apply industrially and on a large scale the techniques of Thomas Bolsover of Sheffield who devised a method of layering copper with a thin sheet of silver. Sheffield plate was widely employed in the manufacture of all manner of objects, from the handles of cutlery and candlesticks to coffee pots, salvers, and tureens. Early Sheffield plate, from 1742 to 1760, was usually tinned on the inner surface, but thereafter silver was applied to both sides. It continued to be fashionable until the 1820s when silver became available in great abundance once more, and it was finally killed off by electroplating which provided a much cheaper and more effective substitute from about 1850 onward.

The Prince of Wales, later King George IV, became Regent in 1811 as a result of the madness of his father who lingered on till 1820. George IV reigned for a decade in his own right and was succeeded by his brother William IV (1830–37). It is convenient, however, to regard this entire period as Regency in terms of style. The Prince Regent's London residence was Carlton House whose interior decoration was entrusted to the architect Henry Holland. Relying largely on French émigré craftsmen, Holland furnished Carlton House in a style which blended classical lines with sumptuous decoration. To this day "Carlton House" is a generic term to describe all manner of furniture in this neoclassical style. Under the influence of such arbiters of taste as Thomas Hope, furniture gradually became more robust, with greater emphasis on comfort than fragile elegance. In addition to the Oriental and gothic motifs of an earlier generation such diverse motifs as balloons, classical friezes, and Egyptian elements (inspired by the discovery of the Rosetta Stone and a new-found craze for the archaeology of the Pharaohs) began to make themselves felt. Exotic timbers, especially from the East Indies, became fashionable.

These influences spilled over into ceramics, silver, and glass. Ormolu gilding and Boulle marquetry, pioneered in France, added a touch of the exotic to furniture and all manner of decorative objects. An interesting development in this period was papier-maché, pioneered by Messrs Jennens & Bettridge of Birmingham, to produce small articles ranging from picture and mirror frames to trays and pole-screens. It involved many sheets of paper glued together under great pressure then kiln-dried and lacquered with mother-of-pearl inlay and gilding for decorative effect. At its zenith, around mid century, papier-maché even extended to chests, chairs, and tables.

Regency fashions did not die out abruptly with the accession of William IV in 1830, but already great social and political changes were sweeping over Britain. Although they were not crystallized until the middle of the century, it is customary in the world of fashion to speak of the Victorian era as if it had commenced seven years before the young queen ascended the throne in 1837. While fashion in ceramics, glass, and silver did not change much before the Great Exhibition of 1851, the styles, techniques, and even the materials of furniture had been undergoing radical alteration in previous decades. The rapid growth of economic prosperity, which came in the 1830s, stimulated a tremendous demand for furniture.

Overnight the traditional craft of furniture making was transformed into a major industry. Mechanical devices and the labor saving techniques of mass production were introduced to accelerate output. Unfortunately furniture in that period did not lend itself well to mass production and inevitably the standards of craftsmanship, and the

enduring qualities which one looks for in good cabinet-making, were sacrificed in the process.

Because the traditional timbers, oak, beech, elm, yew, walnut, and imported hardwoods like mahogany and rosewood, were not really suitable for mechanised furniture making, pine and other softwoods were used increasingly, especially for cheap, painted furniture. This was also the era in which the retail furniture supplier emerged, who bought vast quantities of chairs, tables, beds, and wardrobes from the wholesalers who, in turn, got them from the factory. The direct contact between the furniture maker and the consumer was almost totally eliminated. This pattern of furniture production and distribution has continued down to the present day and was economically inevitable.

The old method of direct contact between manufacturer and consumer was not entirely extinguished. Where it survived, the best traditions of custom-built pieces were maintained, and examples of furniture made to a specific order after 1830 may be as interesting and desirable to the connoisseur as anything produced before that date. It is interesting to note that American furniture, which in colonial times and for half a century thereafter had slavishly followed the styles of the erstwhile mother country, and relied heavily on English imports, now began to develop along distinctive lines, and before the century was out would be exerting its own influence on style. The Shaker furniture of the 19th century, in fact, would have a seminal effect on the developments of the 20th century in which form and functionalism took priority over ornament.

Victorian silver, characterized as so much else from that ebullient era by its extravagant and ostentatious use of decoration, was arguably the most derided and despised aspect of the 19th century applied arts. Silver was the most important status symbol of the Victorian period and, for those who could afford it, it was impossible to have too much of a good thing. As a result of the discovery of vast silver deposits in America and Australia the output of the raw material increased enormously to meet the demand

Above: A French giltwood and Aubusson tapestry upholstered canape from the 19th century.

created by rising prosperity in the United States, Britain, and western Europe. The period from 1830–1900 was a boom time for the silver industry. The restrained classicism of the silver produced in the Regency period, exemplified by the earlier works of Paul Storr and the other great artist-craftsmen of the time, gave way in the 1830s to the Rococo revival. In place of simple gadrooning and Egyptian ornament, came the asymmetrical lines and scrollwork of the Rococo style but, as so often the case in revivals, the craze for rocaille was taken to extremes.

The straightforward acanthus leaf motif of Regency silver gave way to trailing vines and a veritable tangle of scrollwork. Bases became massive and rock-like and the emphasis was laid on the weight or massy appearance of the object. Here and there, however, were examples of simple yet elegant pieces, mainly table wares, and these have generally held their value better than the fussy centerpieces and presentation pieces.

Although Victorian is used as a generic term for the applied and decorative arts of the 19th century it had its European counterparts. The Biedermeier furniture and decor of mid-19th century Germany was long derided—indeed, the term was derived from a fictional character, Gottlieb Biedermeier, a rather simple-minded, essentially philistine petit-bourgeois—as conventional and unimaginative, but today its very solidity is now regarded as highly commendable, while there is much to delight the eye in many of the lesser pieces, especially the ceramics, glass, and silver. The French equivalent was Second Empire, roughly contemporary with the reign of Napoleon III (1852–71), and likewise unfairly dismissed by the generations that followed immediately.

As the 19th century drew to a close, influences and developments in the applied and decorative arts became much more cosmopolitan. The French expression *fin de siecle* has come to be synonymous with decadence. The aestheticism expressed by Oscar Wilde, J.K. Huysmans, and Robert de Montesquieu had its parallels all over Europe and even extended to America. The strange, exotic, luxuriant, and faintly decadent spirit of the times had its flowering in the sinuous lines of Art Nouveau. It was a period of eclecticism, when artists and designers drew freely on all the artistic styles and movements of previous generations from every part of the world, and often jumbled them together in a riotous compote. The craze for Japanese art and artifacts was predominant, but inspiration was also derived from the ancient civilisations of Greece and Rome, Persia, India, Peru, Mexico, Benin, and China. Nevertheless, it is significant that the German term for the turn of the century developments in the arts was Jugendstil or "youth style," implying vigour, freshness, originality, and modernity. The followers of the Arts and Crafts Movement, on the one hand, rejected modern mass production techniques and sought to return to first principles, to handicrafts and inspiration from nature; the disciples of Jugendstil, on the other hand, did not spurn the machine if it could be used to their advantage, and they looked forward, in an age of speed and light, to producing works which would express the qualities of the age.

The major countries of Western Europe and the United States each had an important part to play in the development of the applied and decorative arts. In Britain, the desire for improvement in industrial design can be traced back to the Great Exhibition of 1851 and, even earlier, to the Royal Commission on the Fine Arts in 1835. The Gothic Revival of the mid 19th century stimulated interest in medievalism, reflected in the religious overtones of the early work of William Morris, Philip Webb, and Edward Burne-Jones. It would be difficult to overestimate the importance of Morris to the artistic development of Britain in the late 19th century. Two important movements stemmed directly or indirectly from his teachings, the Arts and Crafts Movement of the 1880s which aimed at bringing artists and craftsmen closer together, to raise standards of workmanship and to put artistic pride into even the most mundane articles, and the Aesthetic Movement, founded on an elitist principle which genuinely strove to raise standards of design and taste. On the continent of Europe, the styles which culminated in Art Nouveau had their origins in France where two major artistic movements flourished in the last third of the century, Naturalism and Symbolism. There were parallel developments in Belgium, Italy, and Spain which fused in the 1890s, were enthusiastically adopted in England and given a distinctly British flavour before finding their way back across the Channel in the guise of *le style anglais*.

The Civil War of 1861–65 was no less traumatic for the United States than the German occupation and the Commune of 1870–71 were for France. The rapid expansion of industry, coupled with widespread immigration from Europe, changed the character of the country in the last three decades of the century. America ceased to be a pioneer land and in the aftermath of the Spanish-American War of 1898 assumed an imperial role. In the arts, as in politics, America now reached out to every part of the globe. Interest in the arts of China and Japan, of Latin America and Africa, were combined with the traditional styles which were themselves derived from the

British, Dutch, and German of the colonial era or imported with the waves of European migration from the 1860s onward. This blend of Oriental or pre-Columbian influences with the styles and techniques of Europe could be seen in the furniture, glassware, and ceramics of America at the turn of the century. These, especially art glass and studio pottery, found their way to Europe where they exerted a considerable influence on the applied arts of the present century.

The young architects and designers of the Chicago School revolutionized the design of buildings and furniture from the 1890s onward. In Europe, the break with the old ideas was often more dramatic as, for example, in the Sezession movement in Austria and Germany. The world of arts and crafts was thrown into turmoil. Many new ideas and styles appeared; some were short-lived and have now become crystallized in the history of the period, but others contained the seeds that germinated in the 1920s and came to full maturity nearer the present day, notably the Bauhaus movement in Germany which influenced the development of Art Deco in the 1920s, with its rejection of the curvilinear extravagance of Art Nouveau. Geometric forms and bright primary colors were in tune with the Jazz Age. Many new forms emerged in the interwar period; the cigarette lighter and the powder compact replaced the snuff box and vinaigrette of earlier generations as ornamental objects which have since become eminently collectable.

While the main collectable categories through the different styles and periods have concentrated on furniture, ceramics, silver, and glass, it should be noted that many other, minor categories emerged mainly in the 19th and 20th centuries and now merit the serious attention of collectors. Although medieval textiles, mainly in the form of needlework, occasionally turn up, the great bulk of material in this category consists of costume from the 18th century onward, with the emphasis on items of apparel from the late 19th and 20th centuries. While clocks and barometers, for practical collecting purposes, exist from the early 18th century onward, relatively few scientific instruments available to the collector predate 1800. Watches, cameras, and optical instruments are even later in origin. Glass paperweights, often produced with the odds and ends left over at the end of the day, have only been around for about a century and half. Few children's playthings date before 1800; the majority of dolls and mechanical toys that now pass through the salesrooms date from 1850 while teddy bears go back no further than the early 1900s. In recent years new categories have attracted a wide following and range from car mascots and aviation memorabilia to golfing, angling, and other sporting collectables.

Pitfalls and Plus Factors

Collectors, and not always beginners by any means, are often puzzled by the vast price differential between two objects which are superficially similar. In some cases there may be as many as a dozen criteria governing the value of an object: age, materials, type of construction, quality of craftsmanship, artistic or aesthetic considerations, unusual technical or decorative features, the provenance of personal association, the presence or absence of makers' marks, full hallmarks, dates, and inscriptions. These and other criteria vary in importance from one object to another, and may even vary within the range of a single category, at different periods or in certain circumstances. Visiting museums and stately homes or handling actual objects at sale previews, as well as studying all the available specialist literature on any given subject, will help the aspiring collector to get a feel for the subject, but there is no short cut to gaining expertise.

Above all, condition is the most problematic factor in assessing the worth of an object. Reasonable condition, of course, depends on the object and the degree to which damage and repairs are accepted by specialist collectors and dealers. A very fine early paneled chair might well have a replacement to the last two inches of a back leg and, if well done, this would have practically no effect on the price. On the other hand, a run-of-the-mill lacquer object, scratched and crudely repainted, would be almost valueless. The general rule is that where a piece is interesting and few collectors have one in their collection, a much damaged example will fetch a surprisingly good price. This often happens with early examples of ceramics from important factories, whereas a common jug, missing a handle, will be virtually worthless. The failure to appreciate the effects on value of poor condition, which of course includes lack of patination, loss of original surface, fading, fraying, or rubbing, is one of the most common causes of the misunderstanding that arise between collectors and dealers.

The market value will also take into account the imponderables of where, when, and how an article came on to the market. There is often a wide disparity in the sum which identical objects may fetch in a London salesroom, in a provincial auction, or a country house sale. The individual vagaries of obsessiveness of two or more wealthy private collectors may grossly affect the auction prices of certain objects on a particular occasion, while absolutely identical objects can (and sometimes do) fetch half these sums at other times in other places. Moreover, there is both a greater disparity between prevailing auction realisations and dealers' retail prices in general, and between the prices of one dealer and another—not always miles apart! Unfortunately, the collector cannot do as the housewife does, and shop around before making a purchase. There are still bargains to be picked up; but all too often one finds that objects are outrageously overpriced in general antique or junk shops. Contrary to popular belief, some of the keenest bargains are still to be found in metropolitan antique shops and markets, where competition comes into play; conversely some of the most atrocious overpricing has been observed in provincial towns or the antique boutiques in tourist areas. There is no clearly definable regional pattern of pricing in the United Kingdom or the United States or anywhere else for that matter; this is something which collectors have to explore themselves.

While a certain amount of judicious repair and restoration is permissible, fakery is reprehensible and usually detracts from whatever value the genuine part of the object may have had before it was tampered with. Unfortunately the dividing line between legitimate repair and outright faking is often a rather tenuous one, but the general principle is that any deliberate altering of an object to create something of greater value is a form of fraud. It occurs most often in furniture where large but unfashionable and unsaleable pieces are dismembered and their timbers used to recreate small pieces which, with a bit of luck, can be passed off as genuine articles. The other problem which besets the unsuspecting collector is reproduction. During the Gothic Revival of the early 19th century some cabinetmakers produced passable reproductions of Jacobean oak and these sometimes present a problem. As a rule, however, the tools used in planing or cutting the timber, or the methods of joining, even where some attempt is made to copy the original, are the factors which reveal the truth. In any case, early Victorian reproductions of earlier styles are now regarded as antiques in their own right, although there will obviously be quite a wide difference in the antiquarian value. So too with early 20th century reproductions of Louis Quinze.

In porcelain it is often a greater problem especially where such factories as Meissen, Derby, or Worcester revive old patterns. Generally speaking, however, variations in marking help to distinguish between the originals and the revivals. In all such cases of doubt, it is recommended that the would-be purchaser get the advice of a reputable dealer or auctioneer. Legislation in many countries in recent years, such as the Trades' Descriptions Act in Britain, place a grave responsibility on the vendors and their agents to ensure that articles are properly described.

At the end of the day, the age-old maxim *caveat emptor* is as important as ever, but do not let this deter you from enjoying the quest for your chosen subject. All collectors make mistakes along the way but so long as they learn from the experience no great harm is done.

Stools and chairs

Stools were the rudimentary forms of low seating with neither back nor armrests and standing on three or four feet which provided the main seating in the Middle Ages and continued to do so well into the 17th century. Thereafter they continued to be useful and convenient types of occasional seating. The early, all-wood type is often referred to as the joint or joined stool, because of its use of the mortise and tenon joint form of construction. Joint stools were fashionable from the 16th to late 17th centuries and were revived in the 19th century as part of the cult of medievalism. They were characterized by plain wooden tops with a simple molding round the edge, turned legs braced by stretchers fixed near the bottom of each leg, and by their overall sturdy construction. The zenith of stool-making was the 18th century when elegant stools with upholstered seats were carved and decorated in the contemporary furniture styles. A much wider range developed from the mid 18th century onward and included foot stools, dressing-table stools, window stools, gout stools (with a raked top for sufferers to rest their legs), closed stools whose hinged seat concealed a chamber pot, and box stools containing a coal-box.

Chairs of one form or another have been used by man since earliest times but as far as the collector is concerned the earliest available types date from the early 17th century. Paneled back chairs with solid backs and seats made with mortise and tenon joints and panels were in vogue till the mid 17th century and continued to be made in country districts well into the 18th century. The back was often decorated with carving on several panels. The legs were usually part-turned with four stretchers joining the legs just above the floor. These chairs were made for the head of the house and the rest of the people round refectory tables would sit on joint stools or log benches.

Square-shaped upholstered chairs, with or without arms, developed from about 1620 and were covered in padded leather secured by large brass-headed nails. An open-backed variety had vertical columns of turning in

Left: George III style mahogany and marquetry Carlton House desk, circa 1900.

bobbin form or a cane back. From about 1665 to 1700, chairs tended to have richly carved high backs with fretted panels. By 1705 the cabriole leg was coming into fashion and the chair back was usually well shaped. From 1750 to 1775 the Chippendale was the height of fashion, characterized by the highly decorated splat usually in a series of curves. A high degree of Rococo was favored, though country versions tend to be much simpler in design. Neoclassical styles (1775–1800) favored lyre, honeysuckle, foliage, wheat ears, and shells for marquetry decoration. Hepplewhite popularized curved backs with shield or oval shapes, whereas Sheraton favored a squarer form of chair. The early 19th century saw Egyptian styles and sabre legs. Back rails became thinner and curved by mid century.

Settles, settees, and sofas

These terms denote any form of seating for two or more people, with arms and a back. Although they are often used indiscriminately, they represent three quite distinct forms of furniture which developed separately.

Settles were the first to evolve, in the mid 15th century when a high wooden back and arms were fitted to long chests. A parallel development was the church pew which retained such medieval features as Gothic tracery and linenfold panels well into the 19th century. Indeed, many examples of this pattern but with a much later date survive to this day in country churches. Oak settles from the late Jacobean period occasionally turn up in the salesroom but fetch high prices. Examples in the Queen Anne and early

Georgian styles are more plentiful, but the majority of pieces now available date from 1750 to 1800, recognized by their cabriole legs. As a result of the Romantic Revival, reproductions of late Jacobean settles were manufactured in Victorian times. They can usually be detected by techniques such as machine planing and a tendency to overdo the carved ornament. Many settles of the 18th and early 19th centuries were made of pine for the cheaper end of the market, but the better examples, especially those with a bowed back, now fetch high prices.

Settees developed in the late 17th century, either as a chair backed form of settle or as a fusion of two armchairs. The latter attained great popularity in the early 18th century and has been much reproduced ever since. The back and seat were upholstered in tapestry but there was great diversity of styling in the back rail, arms, and legs, according to prevailing fashions.

The sofa, based on Turkish and Arabic forms, was introduced into Europe in the 17th century and developed into a long, fully-upholstered seat for reclining or lounging. By the end of the 18th century the sofa was distinguished by its heavily padded back, arms, and seat. The most desirable examples were upholstered in tapestry in the French fashion, and this pattern prevailed through much of the 19th century. Lower down the scale was the Chesterfield sofa with leather buttoned upholstery. The European equivalent was the massive German sofa which characterized the Biedermeier era.

Mid-Victorian variants included the confidante, a sofa consisting of two padded seats facing in different directions. There was also a swivelling version known as a sociable which enabled sitters to turn their seats toward each other. The Knole sofa had movable ends which could be lowered to convert the sofa into a daybed. The chaise longue first made its tentative appearance in the Regency period as a scroll-end sofa but came to full fruition in Victorian times. These elegant pieces are relatively undervalued, compared with the ottoman, a circular sofa with a high curved back. In recent years sofas of the interwar period have risen sharply in value if they exhibit pronounced Art Deco features.

Tables and desks

Refectory tables are the earliest form of table available to the collector, the majority coming to the market dating from 1660. There is a very wide divergence in price between genuine late 17th century tables in fine condition, pieces which have been extensively restored and Victorian reproductions which were fashionable between 1840 and 1870. Generally speaking, the Victorian copies had more elaborate decoration, especially on the legs. Refectory tables were usually made of oak, but elm, yew, walnut, and pearwood were also used in the early 18th century. Draw-leaf tables were devised in the 16th century but did not become common till the 17th century. Thereafter, they followed the various styles in furniture. Gate-leg and folding tables came into fashion in the early 18th century and have continued to this day. They may be found in many different woods and styles and can usually be dated fairly accurately according to the form and structure as well as decorative features. Dining tables developed in the 18th century as drop-leaf or extending tables, sometimes with detachable centerpieces or ends. They have continued to the present day, often reviving classical styles, though the method of construction and timbers employed are usually indicative of the period in which they were made.

Smaller tables include the breakfast table, a pedestal type with a tip-up top, fashionable about 1770 to 1850 and found in walnut, mahogany, or rosewood. Tea-tables with a tripod base evolved in the same period. Card tables and games tables were very popular in the late 18th and 19th centuries. They were often fitted with folding tops so that they could be pushed up against a wall as occasional tables when not in use. The Pembroke table allegedly takes its name from the Countess of Pembroke and is a small drop-flap table with a shallow drawer underneath. The Sutherland table was a much lighter, more elegant form invented in 1850, characterized by a very narrow central section and two large side flaps, which took up little room when not in use. Sofa tables are small drop-flap tables originally intended to stand in front of a sofa for reading or writing and therefore generally fitted with a pedestal base.

Desks evolved out of the writing slopes used by medieval monks, but from the collector's viewpoint they begin with the kneehole desk developed in the late 17th century. By 1750 they were being superseded by pedestal desks with separate top and side sections fitted with drawers. Partners' desks are large desks with drawers at both back and front, enabling two people to share the desk, face to face. Library tables were designed for writing and had drawers underneath the top. As the 18th century progressed they became more elaborate, with tiers of smaller drawers along the back of the top. Rent tables were octagonal, polygonal, or circular 'drum' shapes with small drawers all round for tenants' rent. Smaller drum-shaped tables developed in the early 19th century for the drawing room.

Bureaus, bookcases, and cabinets

The bureau evolved out of the medieval writing slope or lectern, to which was added a small chest of drawers for the storage of writing materials and books. The earliest examples, dating from the late 17th century, were, in fact, produced in two separate sections, the sloping top section and the chest of drawers, often fitted together by heavy beading. This decorative feature was retained in the 18th century, even though bureaus were by that time constructed as a single unit. By 1710 the bureau had developed into its familiar form, with a sloping front which opened up and folded down to form a writing surface. When open, it revealed a bank of drawers or compartments for filing papers and writing implements.

Bureaus of many kinds were in fashion throughout the 19th century and included types with a small glass-fronted bookcase surmounting the sloping top. They may be found in all manner of timbers fashionable in each period, though the most desirable examples are those which were japanned in the early 18th century.

From about 1750 onward, a separate development appeared—the secretaire in which the top drawer of a chest opens out to form the writing flap. When closed, secretaires resemble chests of drawers and lack the characteristic sloping or rounded top of the bureau. They remained popular throughout the 18th and 19th centuries and may be found in many styles and timbers. Likewise, they were often fitted with small bookcases.

Bookcases developed in the late 17th century as open-fronted chests to store books upright. From the outset they were fitted with shelves and close-fitting glazed lids. They remained fairly simple in construction and small in size till about 1740 when they gradually became larger and much more elaborate. Thereafter they followed the general fashions in woods, veneers, and styles, although it is often possible to date a bookcase by the glazing bars and shape of the glass panels. From about 1820 wire grilles were often fitted to allow air to circulate. Circular "drum" or revolving bookcases developed in the 1780s, while square revolving bookcases appeared about a century later.

Among the most elaborate forms of furniture ever made are cabinets, designed to house one's treasures and therefore often objects of great beauty in their own right. Not only do they represent the acme of the cabinetmaker's art but also they were often lavishly decorated with marquetry panels, lacquer or japanning, ormolu, boulle, or carved giltwood. From about 1735 they were fitted with glazed doors and sides for display purposes. Classical styles, such as the Louis Quinze vitrine, were frequently reproduced in Victorian times. Side cabinets include the massive credenza, originating in Italy and developed in France and the Netherlands but attaining immense popularity in the mid 19th century, and the chiffonier, a small cabinet with open shelves developed in the early nineteenth century, but later often fitted with upholstered doors.

Small furniture
The exigencies of space in modern houses have forced many collectors to limit their interests to small pieces. Fortunately there is enormous scope, though it should be noted that demand for small furniture is proportionately higher than for the very large pieces.

The *bonheur du jour* (literally "happiness of the day") is the apt name for a small writing desk fashionable in pre-revolutionary France. The table is surrounded by a tiny cabinet containing drawers, a small bookcase, and pigeon-hole compartments. The most attractive examples were beautifully inlaid in kingwood and satinwood. Commodes are small chests of drawers, usually fitted with twin doors. With its fine decorative inlays and veneered surfaces this elegant piece of furniture was a useful addition to the drawing room. The davenport was a slope-topped desk mounted on a narrow chest with drawers at the sides, invented by a Captain Davenport and originally intended as a portable piece of furniture. The *etagère* consists of tiers of open shelves supported by posts. They vary from simple tiers in walnut or mahogany to those richly decorated with ormolu and have been fashionable since the early 18th century.

Firescreens were once indispensable features of the drawing room in the days of roaring log fires which gave out a fierce heat. They were placed in front of the fire to screen the occupants of the room from scorching. They vary considerably in size, from the large cheval glasses to the diminutive but elegant pole screens, in materials used, from wood, glass, and papier mâché to metals of different kinds. Glass firescreens were often embellished with pictures painted on them or laid on in embroidery.

Bedside tables and night stands vary considerably in shape and composition, from small chests of drawers with a tray top to simple cabinets on tall turned legs designed to contain a chamber pot. The best examples were produced in the late 18th century, but early 19th century types tended to be smaller and this factor lends them charm. After 1830 European bedside cabinets became much larger and more elaborate. They were often produced en suite with small dressing tables and matched sets are now much sought after. The lowboy developed in the early Georgian period as a writing desk or dressing table, with a sloping top mounted on a small chest of drawers. This style returned to fashion in the 1920s and many fine pieces were produced in walnut in the interwar period, but can generally be distinguished from the originals by their machine finish and the addition of mirrors.

Washstands, once an indispensable feature of well-appointed bedrooms, were made of walnut, mahogany, or pine and fitted with a marble top and often a tiled splashback. They were popular throughout the 19th and early 20th centuries, the most desirable examples having Art Nouveau majolica tiling. Pine washstands were originally painted and decorated with floral ornament, but the craze for stripped pine in more recent years has resulted in much of this original work disappearing.

Small upright mirrors mounted on swivels between vertical supports with a drawer or bank of drawers underneath came into fashion at the beginning of the 18th century and sat on dressing tables or tallboys. The style of these toilet mirrors usually parallels that of the wall mirrors of the corresponding period. Examples with japanned woodwork are particularly desirable. Cheval glasses are mirrors on swivel mounts without the base cabinet found in toilet mirrors. They may be quite small and mounted on bracket feet for display on top of a dressing table, and the majority date from 1750 onward.

Oak Bench

late 17th century

At a Glance

Date: Late 17th century
Origin: England
Brief description: An oak bench on turned legs with a padded seat covered in brown leather.

By this time, a concession to creature comfort was provided by the rectangular padded seat covered in close-nailed brown leather, while the turned legs are given greater rigidity by means of square channeled stretchers. The basic style had been fashionable since the late Middle Ages, but upholstery and other refinements reveal its late 17th-century manufacture. Despite its age, such pieces are not as expensive as furniture of a comparable size but a later century.

George I Wing Armchair
early 18th century

At a Glance

Date: Early 18th century
Origin: England
Brief description: A George I walnut wing armchair, previously part of the Donaldson and Griffiths collections.

This ratchet-back chair has a slightly arched top, outscrolled arms, bowed seat, and cabriole legs. Previously in the Donaldson and Griffiths collections, it was purchased by Mrs Peggy Oppenheimer in 1939 for £240 and sold half a century later for almost 140 times as much which, even allowing for inflation in the intervening period, represented an excellent return on the original outlay.

George II Stool
mid 18th century

At a Glance

Date: Mid 18th century
Origin: England
Brief description: A George II walnut stool with cabriole legs and a drop-in seat covered in blue silk damask.

The rounded rectangular drop-in seat is covered in blue silk damask. The cabriole legs are headed by scallop shells and with scroll angles on claw and ball feet. The term "cabriole" is derived from the Latin word capra (a goat), from a fancied resemblance of such furniture legs to the hindleg of a wild goat. This style absolutely dominated furniture from the late 17th century onward, although by the time these stools were made it was beginning to decline in popularity.

George III Stools
c.1770

At a Glance

Date: c.1770
Origin: England
Brief description: A pair of
   George III mahogany
   stools.

*This pair is characterized by
serpentine upholstered
rectangular seats covered in
salmon patterned silk above
a conforming apron carved
with a central patera issuing
bellflower garlands. The
cabriole legs have scrolled
feet and the frames are
grooved overall.*

George III Open Armchairs
c. 1780

At a Glance

Date: c.1780
Origin: England
Brief description: A pair of
George III mahogany
open armchairs with
cartouche-shaped
padded backs and
tapering legs.

*Each chair has a channeled
cartouche-shaped padded
back, with part-padded arms
and leaf-wrapped ball
terminals, on forward-swept
fluted supports and
anthemion-headed fluted
tapering legs. These elegant
chairs in the French cabriolet
manner were designed in the
French-Grecian style
associated with John Linnell
(1729–96), author of A New
Book of Ornaments (1760).
Chairs in this style have been
documented from that
decade, but this particular
pair was made for Inveraray
Castle, Scotland, after a
Linnell pattern in the 1780s.*

Chippendale Bergère
c. 1770

The arched back, padded sides, and seat are upholstered in a patterned fabric. The central crest is carved with a beribboned laurel enclosing a beaded patera. The bowed reed seat rail is mounted on circular tapering and fluted legs ending in beaded stiff-leaf carved feet. This chair was made by Thomas Chippendale (1718–79), a native of Otley, Yorkshire, who established a workshop in London in 1754, the year in which he published The Gentleman and Cabinet-maker's Director, *the first furniture trade catalog. Chippendale achieved a high reputation for his fine furniture in the neoclassical style.*

Louis XVI Marquises
c. 1780

At a Glance

Date: c.1780
Origin: France
Brief description: A pair of Louis XVI giltwood marquises made by Georges Jacob of Paris.

Each chair has a stiff-leaf and beaded rectangular upholstered back, with padded arms and guilloché carved scrolled terminals leading to acanthus-decorated supports on fluted blocks. The loose cushions are upholstered in a pale blue silk damask, and the seats are raised on rosette-capped, stop-fluted tapering legs. Each is stamped G. Jacob once and B.C. four times. Georges Jacob was a master cabinetmaker in Paris by 1765, and this particular pair of marquises remained in the Jacob family until 1993.

English Windsor Chair
late 19th century

At a Glance

Date: Late 19th century
Origin: England
Brief description: An ash, elm, fruitwood, and beech Windsor Chair.

The best known and most enduringly popular item of country furniture is the Windsor Chair. Whether George IV had some made for Windsor Castle or not (as is often averred) the fact is that these spindle-backed chairs have been made since the mid 17th century, in yew, ash, elm, beech, or willow, in many parts of England from Lancashire to Somerset. This chair is a good example of the most elaborate and substantial of the splat-back Windsor Chairs, produced in High Wycombe by firms such as Glenister and Gibbons.

Louis Philippe Chair
c.1840–45

At a Glance

Date: c.1840–45
Origin: France
Brief description: A Louis Philippe rosewood and marquetry chair by Joseph-Pierre-François Jeanselme.

The chair is inlaid with floral scrolls and lines. The arched padded back and seat is covered in floral green velvet, with scrolling arms, while the cabriole legs terminate in scroll feet. It bears the mark of Joseph-Pierre-François Jeanselme (d.1860) who in 1824 founded a furniture business that continued until 1930. In the mid 19th century, Jeanselme refurnished several palaces, including Fontainebleau and the Palais Royal.

Welby Pugin Side-chairs
c. 1847

At a Glance

Date: c.1847
Origin: England
Brief description: A pair of
early Victorian oak side-chairs
designed by Augustus Welby
Pugin and made for John
Harris, London.

*They have a foliate-carved frame,
brass-nailed leather back flanked
by lions' heads, on x-framed legs
joined by foliate and
geometrically carved stretchers.
The backs are embossed with a
flower-head centered by the
letter H, identifying John Harris
of Prince's Gate, London. These
robust lion-headed oak chairs in
the Gothic style were conceived
for the New Palace of
Westminster by Augustus Welby
Pugin (1812–52). Trained as an
architect under his father, he was
preeminent in the revival of
Gothic styles in building and
furniture in the mid 19th century.*

Mackintosh Chair
1898

At a Glance

Date: 1898
Origin: Scotland
Brief description: A high-
backed oak chair.

This highly distinctive and very desirable chair was designed by the celebrated architect and interior designer, Charles Rennie Mackintosh (1868–1928), who had a tremendous impact on European furniture at the turn of the last century. It is a variant of the chair designed by him for Miss Cranston's Argyle Street Tea Rooms, Glasgow, earlier in 1898. The oval top rail is carved with an apple motif, flanked by tapering finials with solid splats. This was the first Mackintosh chair to reveal the exaggeratedly high back which became almost his trademark.

Bentwood Chairs

1898

At a Glance

Date: 1898
Origin: Austria
Brief description: Two bentwood chairs
   designed by Adolf Loos and made for the
   Café Museum in Vienna by J. and J. Kohn.

They have shaped open backs, rounded cane seats, and slightly tapered legs with U-formed stretchers. Bentwood furniture, constructed from strips of bent and laminated copper beech, was pioneered by the German manufacturer Michael Thonet (1796–1871) about 1830, and after his patent expired in 1869 this technique spread all over Europe. These chairs were designed by Adolf Loos (1870–1933) and made for the Café Museum in Vienna by J. and J. Kohn. Although ideally suited to factory production, these particular chairs were never mass produced.

Majorelle Bergère
c.1900

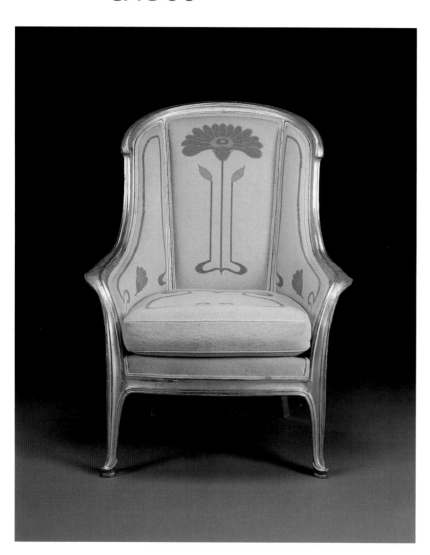

At a Glance

Date: c.1900
Origin: France
Brief description: A giltwood bergère designed by Louis Majorelle.

The back of this yellow-upholstered chair is delicately ornamented with a stylized plant, with matching decoration on the arms. It was designed by Louis Majorelle (1859–1929), one of the leading architects and designers of the Art Nouveau period. After studying art at Paris he took charge of his family's ceramics factory, but from 1879 onward he became more and more involved in the design and manufacture of furniture. About 1890 he came under the influence of Emile Gallé and this led to furniture which laid emphasis on fluid sculptural lines. Gilt mounts, mainly with lily motifs, were virtually Majorelle's trademark from 1900 onward.

Bugatti Chair
c.1900

At a Glance

Date: c.1900
Origin: Italy
Brief description: A beaten metal and
    cane garden chair designed by Carlo
    Bugatti.

*This unusual chair has a bent cane frame
with beaten metal ornament and a high
spindle back decorated with tassels. It is a
rare example of garden furniture
designed by Carlo Bugatti (b.1855).
Originally following in a long family
tradition as a painter, Bugatti began
designing silverware, metalwork, and
furniture in the Art Nouveau idiom.
Although overshadowed by his brilliant
sons, Rembrandt the sculptor (1885–1916)
and Ettore the car designer (1882–1947),
Carlo has come into prominence in recent
years and his furniture is now very much
sought after.*

Gruber Armchairs
c.1903

The broad curved back is carved with stylized foliate motifs and the leather upholstery is secured by close-nailing. They were designed by Jacques Gruber who studied design under Emile Gallé at the Nancy School from 1901 onward, developing his own highly distinctive style which explored plant shapes and forms that tended to become rather ponderous. Although dismissed as provincial for many years, Gruber's furniture has been the subject of reassessment in recent years and the fine quality of the workmanship is now given its due respect.

At a Glance

Date: c.1903
Origin: France
Brief description: A pair of carved walnut upholstered armchairs designed by Jacques Gruber.

Hoffmann and Moser Armchair Frames
c.1905

These armchairs were part of the furniture commissioned for the Purkersdorf
Sanatorium in 1905 and designed by Josef Hoffmann and Koloman Moser,
the two outstanding figures of the Wiener Werkstätte. This pair was gifted
to a former employee of the sanatorium about 1950. Just after World War II
the sanatorium was purchased by an evangelical mission and converted into
a hospital. Much of the original interior was destroyed and its
furniture dispersed.

At a Glance

Date: c.1905
Origin: Austria
Brief description: A pair of
   wooden armchair frames
   designed by Josef Hoffmann and
   Koloman Moser given as a gift to
   a former employee of the
   Purkersdorf Sanatorium.

Olbrich Armchair
c.1905

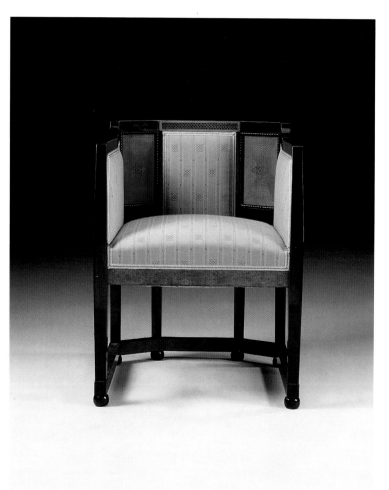

At a Glance

Date: c.1905
Origin: Germany
Brief description: An inlaid and ebonized armchair designed by Joseph Maria Olbrich.

The chair is basically an upholstered tub form with inlaid panels, burrwood stretcher, and bun feet. This chair appears to have been designed to accompany a desk which is now in the Victoria and Albert Museum. It was designed by Joseph Maria Olbrich (1867–1908) who studied in Vienna under Otto Wagner and later joined with Josef Hoffmann to found the Vienna Sezession in 1897. Two years later he joined the artists' colony formed at Darmstadt under the aegis of the Grand Duke Ernst Ludwig of Hesse for whom he designed furniture very similar to this piece.

English Art Nouveau Salon Suite
c.1910

At a Glance

Date: c.1910
Origin: England
Brief description: An English Art
   Nouveau mahogany and inlaid
   seven-piece salon suite.

This salon suite comprises a two-
seater settee, four side-chairs, and
two armchairs, each with a square
slatted back with inlaid wood and
metal stylized motif above a padded
seat on square legs terminating in
pad feet. This is an interesting
example of the transition from the
curvilinear style at the turn of the
century to the more angular pattern
about 1910, under the influence of
Charles Rennie Mackintosh and the
so-called Glasgow School.

Olbrich Furniture

c.1905

A leading light of the Vienna Sezession, Joseph Maria Olbrich (1867–1908) was one of Austria's leading architects who also designed metalwork, jewelry, and furniture, such as this bentwood suite, in the prevailing Jugendstil manner. Olbrich was the architect responsible for the Hofpavillon and the Karlsplatz Bahnhof in Vienna, as well as many of the interior fittings of the Vienna Metropolitan Railway, including a great deal of different pieces in the bentwood medium.

At a Glance

Date: c.1905
Origin: Austria
Brief description: A suite of bentwood furniture designed by Joseph Maria Olbrich comprising a settee, two armchairs, and two side-chairs.

Morris Chair
c.1909

At A Glance

Date: c.1909
Origin: USA
Brief description: An oak chair designed by Gustav Stickley in a style influenced by William Morris.

This armchair, in a style pioneered by William Morris (1834–96) in England, was developed by Gustav Stickley (1857–1942) of New York. Stickley was one of the foremost disciples of the Arts and Crafts Movement, which had crossed the Atlantic in 1876, the year of the Centennial Exposition at Philadelphia, and continued to flourish until 1915 when Stickley went bankrupt. Stickley's furniture was generally made of oak with robust, no-nonsense lines—solid and comfortable but ascetic in character, hence the alternative name of Mission furniture, reminiscent of the Spanish misiones that civilized the Old West.

Frank Lloyd Wright Side-Chair
1916–22

At A Glance

Date: 1916–22
Origin: USA
Brief description: An oak side-chair designed by Frank Lloyd Wright for the Imperial Hotel, Tokyo.

The preeminent American architect of the early 20th century was Frank Lloyd Wright (1869–1959) who trained under Louis Sullivan and subsequently established his own practice in Chicago. Many of the most prestigious buildings in the United States from 1906 onward were either designed by him or strongly influenced by his innovative ideas. As far back as 1894, however, he published his theories on design and put them into practice. Most of his so-called "progressive" oak furniture from the turn of the century onward was made for him by George Niedecken of Milwaukee. This side-chair was one of a set designed by Wright for the Imperial Hotel, Tokyo, between 1916 and 1922.

Ruhlmann Chair
c.1918

At A Glance

Date: c.1918
Origin: France
Brief description: A retombante mahogany chair designed by Emile-Jacques Ruhlmann.

This reclining chair, upholstered in velvet, was designed by Emile-Jacques Ruhlmann (1879–1933), arguably one of the greatest French ébénistes of the 20th century. Like many others of his generation he was extremely versatile and designed fabrics, wallpapers, and ceramics as well as furniture, though it is for the latter that he is best remembered. He made his debut at the Salon d'Automne in 1910 and over the ensuing decade perfected the style which is known nowadays as Art Deco.

Breuer Armchair
c.1922

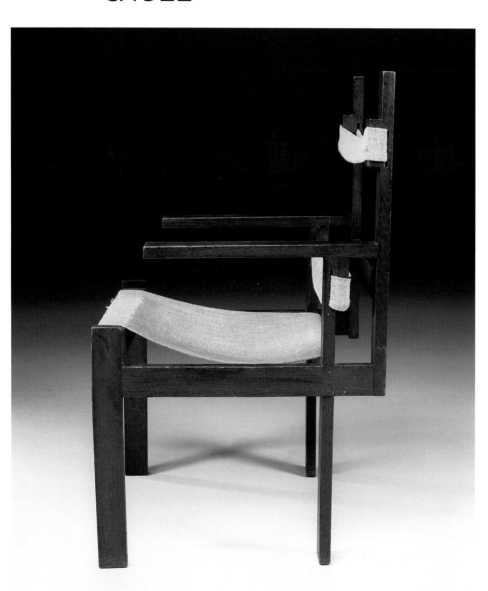

At A Glance

Date: c.1922
Origin: Germany
Brief description: An oak lath armchair designed by Marcel Breuer.

It is of rectilinear construction, incorporating standardized strips of oak, with a slung canvas seat and two canvas back straps. It was designed about 1922 by Marcel Breuer (1902–81), a Hungarian-born designer who trained under Walter Gropius at the original Bauhaus in Weimar in whose workshops this chair and other pieces of furniture by Breuer were first produced. Breuer specialized in designing furniture that was capable of mass production, and many of his designs were subsequently realized by Thonet Brothers in Vienna. Breuer left Germany in 1935 and eventually settled in the USA.

Gray Transat Armchair
1925-6

At A Glance

Date: 1925–6
Origin: France
Brief description: A Transat armchair in black lacquer, steel, and leather, designed by Eileen Gray.

This startlingly modern chair, in black lacquer, chromed steel, and leather, was designed by Eileen Gray (1878–1976), the Irish-born designer who spent most of her working life in France where she established a reputation as the finest exponent of lacquer in furniture. Her earliest sketches for the Transat chair were executed in 1924 but it was not until 1930 that she patented the design. During her long career Gray produced a great deal of ceramics, but she is best remembered for her contribution to Art Deco furniture.

Dieckmann Child's Chair
1928

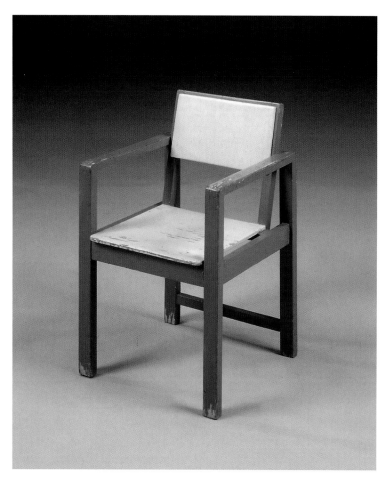

At A Glance

Date: 1928
Origin: Germany
Brief descrption: A blue and cream painted child's chair designed by Erich Dieckmann in cream and blue.

This simple chair has an angled back with a flat panel painted in cream to match the seat, the arms, uprights, and legs being painted bright blue. It was designed by Erich Dieckmann who studied at the Bauhaus in Weimar from 1921 to 1925 and remained in the woodworking shop at Weimar after the Bauhaus moved to Dessau in 1925. From 1926 to 1930 he was the Director of the Bauhochschule at Weimar during which period he produced some of his most successful designs in wood.

Van der Rohe Armchair and Stool
1930

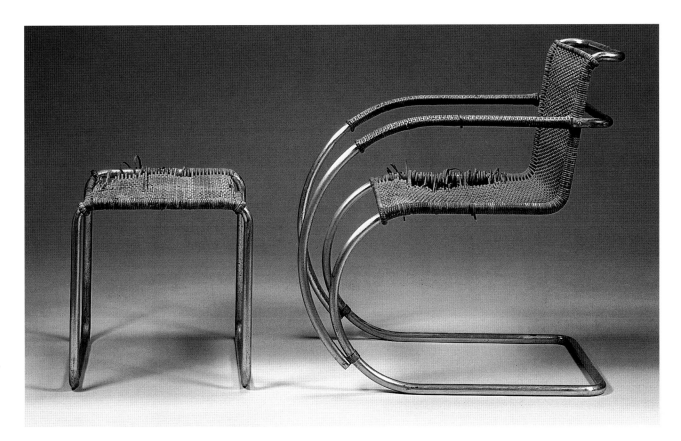

The nickel-plated tubular steel frame has curved arm rails, while the arm-rests and seat are of cane and the stool is made of the same materials. They were designed by Ludwig Mies van der Rohe (1886–1969), an architect and designer who trained at the Bauhaus where he was director from 1930, until he left Germany and settled in the United States in 1938. This chair and matching stool, commissioned by Philip Johnson for his New York apartment, were manufactured by the Joseph Müller metalworks in Berlin, the canework being executed by Lily Reich.

At A Glance

Date: 1930
Origin: Germany
Brief description: A tubular steel armchair and stool designed by Ludwig Mies van der Rohe.

Le Corbusier Wooden Chairs
c.1930

At A Glance

Date: c.1930
Origin: France
Brief description: A pair of adjustable wooden chairs attributed to Le Corbusier for La Maison Savoye at Poissy.

The movable rectangular seat and backrest have wickerwork and leather upholstery studded with large copper nails. The plain rectangular legs, slats, and arm-rests have an almost medieval appearance. This design has been attributed to Le Corbusier, the pseudonym of Charles Edouard Jeanneret (1887–1965). Born in Switzerland, he left school at 13 to become an engraver of watch cases. Self taught in architecture, he produced many highly distinctive designs. Though relatively few were actually brought to fruition they have had a tremendous impact on later generations.

Aalto Armchair
c.1931

At A Glance

Date: c.1931
Origin: Finland
Brief description: A birch and bent plywood armchair designed by Alvar Aalto.

The bent and laminated birch frame supports a stained and lacquered bent plywood seat. The frame was particularly revolutionary at the time, being the first use of laminated wood in a cantilevered leg structure. This extraordinary innovation was the work of the renowned Finnish architect and designer Alvar Aalto (1898–1976) and typifies his flair for harnessing the most modern materials. His impact on furniture design is immense and continues to this day.

Rietveld Easy Chairs and Coffee Table c.1934

At A Glance

Date: c.1934
Origin: Netherlands
Brief description: Two pinewood easy chairs and a matching coffee table designed by Gerrit Rietveld.

The chairs have slatted angled backs and open angled seats between open arm-rests and square uprights, while the table is of slat construction, the top supported by an X-stretcher attached to slatted legs. This suite of crate easy furniture was designed by Gerrit Rietveld (1888–1964), the leading architect and furniture designer of Holland in the interwar period who was strongly influenced by De Stijl movement. He designed the Schröder House in Utrecht (1924) and the Van Gogh Museum in Amsterdam, but his Red-and-Blue Chair (1918) immediately established his reputation as an avant-garde furniture designer.

Breuer Chaise Longue
c.1938

*This unusual piece of
furniture was designed by
Marcel Breuer (1902–81), one
of the most talented
craftsmen to work at the
Bauhaus in Weimar. He took
charge of the Bauhaus
furniture workshop in 1934
and was the first to design
furniture in tubular steel, his
Wassily chair being regarded
as a modern classic. This
model was first produced in
steel by Embru and then
aluminum by Stylclair
of France.*

Eames Lounge Chair
1945

At A Glance

Date: 1945
Origin: USA
Brief description: A laminated birch lounge chair designed by Charles Eames.

The seat and back are of molded birch laminate, mounted on a chromed metal frame with screw-in metal and rubber glides. The frame was subsequently painted black. The transfer label on the underside identifies it as having been made by the Evans Products Company and retailed by the Herman Miller Furniture Company. It was designed by Charles Eames (1907–78), an architect and designer who collaborated with the Finnish-born designer Eero Saarinen (1910–61). Later they would move on from wood laminates to various forms of plastic, developing furniture styles which are in universal use to this day.

George II Hall Bench
c.1735

At a Glance

Date: c.1735
Origin: England
Brief description: A George II mahogany hall bench attributed to William Kent.

The double-arched crest rail is decorated with scrolled acanthus tops above a paneled back with bead-and-reel edge flanked by outscrolled handrests on scrolled acanthus-sheathed legs. This Roman-pattern settee conforms to a design from the 1720s by William Kent (1684–1748), one of those Renaissance men whose influence on design was enormous. An architect, landscape gardener, and designer, he studied the Palladian architecture of Italy in 1709–10 and was one of the foremost proponents of the baroque style in England.

George III Sofa
c.1770

The rectangular padded back and seat are covered in green and gold foliate silk-damask, the downswept arms and legs are carved with Greek key fret, on pierced Chinese paling fretwork stretchers and brass castors. It is believed to have been supplied to Thomas Stapleton of Carlton Hall (now Towers) near Goole, Yorkshire, where it remained until 1992. Although the cabinetmaker who made this outstanding piece is not identified, it has echoes of William Kent and Thomas Chippendale.

At a Glance

Date: c.1770.
Origin: England
Brief description: A George III mahogany sofa possibly by William Kent or Thomas Chippendale.

Regency Daybed
c.1810

The padded scrolling end is covered in white calico, above a reeded seat rail and stands on ring-turned tapering legs fitted with brass caps and castors. Grecian sofas of this design are illustrated in the Cabinet Encyclopaedia published in 1804 by Thomas Sheraton (1751–1806), showing a similar reed-enriched frame and a couch with tapering columnar stump feet and scroll-cushioned ends which typifies the elegant neoclassical furniture associated with his name.

At a Glance

Date: c. 1810
Origin: England
Brief description: A Regency mahogany Grecian sofa.

Regency Mahogany Daybed
c.1815

At a Glance

Date: c.1815
Origin: England
Brief description: A Regency mahogany daybed that was possibly supplied to the Prince Regent for Cumberland Lodge, Windsor Park, England.

The serpentine side-rest is carved with Greek key pattern extending to the top, with paneled sides, shaped back rest, and scrolled terminal and paw support. It stands on reeded patera-headed sabre legs. This piece bears the evidence of having been altered at a subsequent period. It was probably supplied to the Prince Regent (later George IV) for Cumberland Lodge, Windsor Park, England, and remained there till at least 1872. This pattern also appears in Sheraton's Encyclopaedia *and is very similar to a round-end Grecian sofa supplied to the Prince's Carlton House in 1807.*

William IV Back Settee

c.1836

The undulating foliate back scroll has reeded finials and pierced fret-carved tendrils. The settee stands on fluted uprights with spirally turned splats, while the padded arms have swan's head terminals. The padded seat rests on a base with reeded, turned, and tapered legs, fitted with brass caps and castors. It is richly carved in the "Old English" style fashionable in the early 19th century, but the overall style of the settee was inspired by a Coromandel chair imported from India by the Bond Street dealer John Webb and which was illustrated by H. Shaw in Specimens of Ancient Furniture *(1836).*

At a Glance

Date: c.1836
Origin: England
Brief description: A William IV rosewood triple-chair back settee in the "Old English" style.

Louis Philippe *Banquettes de Billiard*
c. 1847

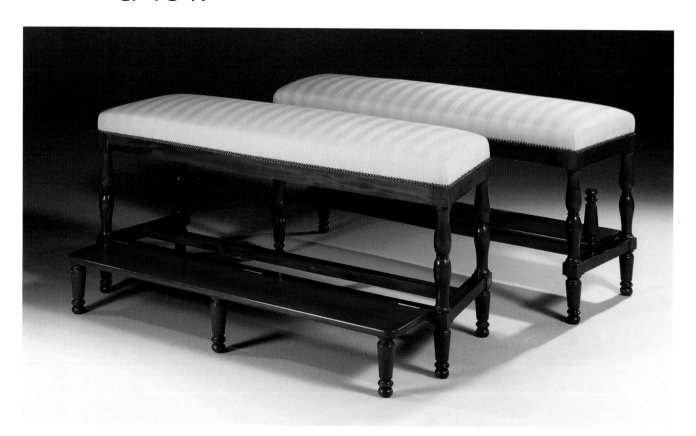

At a Glance

Date: c.1847
Origin: France
Brief description: A pair of Louis Philippe mahogany *banquettes de billiard*, which bear the mark of the Jeanselme family.

Each has a spreading rectangular seat covered in close-nailed yellow upholstery by Ancelot. It stands on turned baluster supports above a hinged step on turned tapering legs. These benches were intended to stand at the sides of billiard rooms giving spectators a slightly elevated view of the game. They bear the mark of the Jeanselme family which established their workshop on the Rue du Harley in 1840. Seven years later they purchased the workshop and stock of the Jacob family and it is believed that these banquettes emanated from that source.

French Chaise Longue

c.1885

The floral and beribboned carved frame has a scrolled back and acanthus-clasping arm-rest supported by winged putti. The padded back, arm-rest, and oblong seat cushion are covered in floral apricot damask, and the chaise rests on stop-fluted ionic columnar legs. This model was exhibited at the Paris Exposition of 1878 by the well-known Parisian firm of Fourdinois, drawing a favorable comment from the Art Journal which described it as "graceful and beautiful, the composition having exercised a brilliant fancy."

At a Glance

Date: c.1885
Origin: France
Brief description: A giltwood chaise longue exhibited at the Paris Exposition of 1878 by Fourdinois.

Ruhlmann Sofa
c.1925

At a Glance

Date: c.1925
Origin: France
Brief description: An upholstered
Macassar ebony sofa designed by
Emile-Jacque Ruhlmann.

Technically speaking a sofa is any movable seat on which to recline.
Nowadays the term seems to be almost synonymous with settee, but
originally it meant a much softer and more comfortable piece of
furniture, inspired by the heavily upholstered dais on which the Grand
Vizier of the Ottoman Empire conducted affairs of state. Interestingly, the
divan, a long, low, backless couch has a somewhat similar derivation,
being originally the privy council of the Ottoman Empire and thus any
council chamber in Islamic countries. This splendid example was created
by Emile-Jacques Ruhlmann (1879–1933) about 1925.

Thonet Bentwood Settee

c.1870

Bentwood furniture was pioneered by Michael Thonet (1796–1871) who began applying techniques for bending and shaping wood to chairs about 1830. In the early decades the furniture was handmade and destined for the palaces and castles of the Central European nobility but, in 1851, this light furniture was supplied to the mass market for the first time. Bentwood furniture first caught the public eye when it was installed in Vienna's Café Daum and Budapest's Queen of England Hotel. Thonet's bentwood furniture marked the beginning of modern design and strongly influenced such diverse designers as Le Corbusier, Marcel Breuer, Alvar Aalto, and Mies van der Rohe.

At a Glance

Date: c.1870
Origin: Germany
Brief description: A bentwood settee designed by Michael Thonet.

Greene & Greene Couch
c.1914

At a Glance

Date: c.1914
Origin: USA
Brief description: A Honduras mahogany couch designed by Charles and Henry Greene.

Upholstered in yellow damask silk, its frame is decorated with ebony details and fully finished book-matched grain panels across the back. It was designed by Charles and Henry Greene and executed in the workshop of Peter Hall for the living room of the Robert R. Blacker House, Pasadena, California. Charles and Henry Greene trained as architects at the Massachusetts Institute of Technology from which they graduated in 1892. About a year later they moved to Pasadena where they began designing houses, interiors, and furniture, often strongly eclectic and deriving inspiration from such disparate sources as Japan and the Franciscan missions of Spanish colonial times.

Majorelle Bedstead
c.1900

This is a splendid example of Louis Majorelle's Art Nouveau furniture at its most florid and flamboyant, the contrasting colors and textures of the two timbers being exploited fully in the carved and applied decoration. The influence of Emile Gallé prevented Majorelle from indulging in the flights of fancy to which so many of his contemporaries of the 1890s were prone. The furniture of Majorelle (1859–1929) reached its peak in the work which he exhibited at the Paris Exposition of 1900. Although it laid emphasis on fluid sculptural forms it was more practical and restrained than that designed by his rival Hector Guimard.

Stickley Bed

c.1905

At a Glance

Date: c.1905
Origin: USA
Brief description: An oak double bed designed by Gustav Stickley.

Oak symbolizes robust integrity and for that reason it was the preferred medium of Gustav Stickley who founded his own company in 1898 after traveling all over Europe studying the latest developments in Arts and Crafts furniture. His own furniture was almost puritanical in its severity and it is significant that he used the brand name "Craftsman" to emphasize its craft-based qualities. Ironically the rival firm of L. &. J.G. Stickley, formed by his brothers Leopold and George, capitalized on the family name in their mass produced furniture, whereas Gustav was forced into liquidation.

English Folding Table
mid 17th century

At a Glance

Date: Mid 17th century
Origin: England
Brief description: An oak folding table on turned legs with a round top above a paneled door.

Such folding tables began to emerge in the late 16th century and were very fashionable in the ensuing century. They were distinguished by a hinged top, which, when closed, presented a semi-circular or triangular surface. This example has a round top above a paneled door with split moldings, on turned legs with block feet and square section stretchers. Such pieces were sometimes called credence tables, alluding to the table by the altar used for storing the host and communion wine before consecration.

English Gateleg Table
mid 17th century

At a Glance

Date: Mid 17th century
Origin: England
Brief description: An oak gateleg table with twin flap top and hinged gates.

This early example has an oval twin flap top and hinged gates, the waved frieze with two end drawers. The slender baluster legs are joined by stretchers on turned feet, a style which came into fashion about 1650 and continued in oak to the end of the century.

Charles II Side Table
c.1675

At a Glance

Date: c.1675
Origin: England
Brief description: A
  Charles II oak side table
  with a paneled front
  showing two simulated
  drawers.

The term side table is usually applied to any table designed to stand against a wall, especially in a dining room where it was a convenient place on which to place the serving dishes. This fine example has a molded rectangular plank top enclosing a well, the paneled front with two simulated drawers. The baluster legs joined by square stretchers on bun feet were especially fashionable in the last quarter of the 17th century.

George II Desk
c.1740

At a Glance

Date: c.1740
Origin: England
Brief description: A George II kingwood kneehole desk in a design inspired by the Palladian mansions of the period.

A kneehole or recess for the legs first appeared in tables in the late 17th century and this was extended to writing desks half a century later. This example has a crossbanded brown leather-lined rectangular top above a central kneehole with foliate and trellis-work border. This type of desk was derived from the dressing table with an arched center flanked by small drawers. Its architectural elements were inspired by the Palladian mansions of the period.

George II Table
c.1750

At a Glance

Date: c.1750
Origin: Ireland
Brief description: A George II mahogany center table that once belonged to a Mrs E. Ball, Dublin.

The rounded rectangular dished top is mounted above a waved frieze with a shell of rather later date on the front and reverse. It stands on cabriole legs terminating in faceted pad feet. The remains of a paper label on the underside indicate that it once belonged to a Mrs E. Ball of 53 Stephen's Green, Dublin. Ephemeral features of this sort can often be very useful in establishing the provenance and period of furniture.

George III Rudd's Table
c.1780

At a Glance

Date: c.1780
Origin: England
Brief description: A George III mahogany Rudd's table once the property of Martin Kalicky of Nieborowie, Poland.

The rectangular top is mounted above a simulated slide and has a pair of small drawers enclosing adjustable mirrors, flanking a central fitted drawer with a ratcheted baize-lined writing surface. The table stands on square tapering legs fitted with brass caps and castors. An inscription on the underside reveals that it was the property of Martin Kalicky of Nieborowie, Poland, in 1878. A lady's dressing table of this pattern is illustrated in Thomas Shearer's The Cabinet-maker's London Book of Prices *(1788) where he states that it was named after Margaret Caroline Rudd who died in 1779.*

George III Pembroke Table
c.1775

At a Glance

Date: c.1775
Origin: England
Brief description: A George III tulipwood and marquetry Pembroke table attributed to Mayhew and Ince.

Small light tables of this type are believed to have been introduced by the Countess of Pembroke (1737–1831) about 1760 and are distinguished by having two drop leaves and one or more shallow drawers beneath the central section. This example has a tulipwood banded oval drop-leaf top, inlaid with a central conch shell within a ruffled shell and green-stained oval reserve which is cornered by engraved ribbon-tied flowering branches. The use of natural colored woods enhanced with engraving and inlaid to produce a striking visual effect is often a signature of the work of Mayhew and Ince. They established their workshop in 1759 in Broad Street, London, and produced furniture for the next 40 years. It is often difficult to attribute firmly their works to them because of their unpredictable variations in style, construction, and quality.

George III Sofa Table
late 18th century

At a Glance

Date: Late 18th century
Origin: England
Brief description: A George III rosewood sofa table inlaid with boxwood and ebonized lines.

The sofa table was a logical development of the Pembroke table, although generally narrower and longer. They were designed to stand alongside sofas so that ladies could write their letters in comfort. This example made from rosewood is inlaid overall with boxwood and ebonized lines, the rounded rectangular twin flap top is crossbanded in satinwood above a pair of part mahogany-lined frieze drawers with a conforming pair of simulated drawers on the reverse.

Carlton House Desk
c.1790

This highly distinctive form derives its name from a desk made originally for Carlton House, the residence of the Prince of Wales (later George IV) and now preserved in Buckingham Palace. Similar examples were appearing in cabinetmakers' catalogs by the mid 1790s. This example is in brass-mounted satinwood, inlaid overall with boxwood and ebonized lines, and crossbanded in tulipwood. The form of the reed-capped columnar legs enriched with flutes and the pierced-brass gallery was popularized by the Prince Regent.

George III Architect's Pedestal Desk
c.1798

At a Glance

Date: c.1798
Origin: England
Brief description: A George III mahogany architect's pedestal desk attributed to Gillow, Lancaster.

The double-ratcheted hinged top is covered with a green leather writing surface and is mounted above a fitted frieze drawer. The lidded compartments are each inlaid with letters of the alphabet above a kneehole flanked by three short graduated drawers. The back has two simulated long drawers above a pair of panels, the whole being set on a plinth base. This very functional pedestal desk has been attributed to Gillow of Lancaster. It was founded by Robert Gillow (1704–92), a humble joiner who rose to become the most successful furniture maker of his generation, and the forerunner of the great department store of Waring & Gillow of London.

Italian Console Table
mid 19th century

This is the name applied to a kind of side table, supported at the front by one or two legs and attached to the wall by means of brackets. This example is in giltwood with a white marble serpentine top. A bird with outstretched wings forms the centerpiece of the elaborate frieze flanked by a foliate festoon supported by cherub caryatids. The scrolled legs joined by an X-shaped stretcher, surmounted by rockwork and shell cartouche amid flowers, are in the finest Rococo tradition.

At a Glance

Date: Mid 19th century
Origin: Italy
Brief description: A console table in giltwood with a white marble serpentine top.

Russian Center Table
mid 19th century

At a Glance

Date: Mid 19th century
Origin: Russia
Brief description: An ormolu-mounted mahogany center table of Empire Style.

This table has an inset circular top above an anthemion and foliate frieze. It has a columnar stem and a tripartite base with female caryatids. The extraordinary decoration of this table consists of ormolu (from French or moulu—ground gold). This technique was devised in France by the middle of the 16th century and originally consisted of cast bronze ornament gilded with an amalgam of mercury and gold, but because it proved to be hazardous to the workmen (who suffered mercury poisoning as a result) it fell into disrepute until the mid 19th century when a much less harmful substitute was produced.

Regency Low Tables
c.1715

At A Glance

Date: c.1715
Origin: France
Brief description: A pair of Regency gilt-gesso stools converted to low tables.

Each rectangular top is decorated with pagodas, trees, rocks, and figures over a shaped frieze with a diaper ground and centered on a shell. The cabriole legs have volute feet and are headed by a rocaille ornament. Originally constructed as a pair of stools, they were converted half a century later into low tables with the addition of Chinese red and gilt lacquer panels, an interesting example of a later generation rejecting the purpose of the original and applying its own taste, changing it to a function more suitable to the period.

Louis XV Coiffeuse
c.1770

At A Glance

Date: c.1770
Origin: France
Brief description: A late Louis XV mahogany coiffeuse with the mark of Jean François Leleu.

The French term comes from the fact that it was the sort of table at which ladies sat while their maids attended to their hair. This example has a shaped rectangular tripartite cleated top, centered by an adjustable flap with a mirror on the reverse. This is flanked by two hinged flaps above a kneehole having two small drawers on either side. The top right-hand drawer has a fitted interior although it lacks the accessories, and the table stands on cabriole legs terminating in upswept sabots of a later vintage. The top left-hand drawer bears the mark of Jean François Leleu who flourished in Paris in the 1760s and 1770s.

Louis XVI-style Lady's Dressing Table
c.1880

At A Glance

Date: c.1880
Origin: France
Brief description: An ormolu-mounted lady's dressing table in the Louis XVI style.

The rectangular top has rounded corners, with a finely cast three-quarter gallery inset with three 17th century Japanese lacquer panels set in a gold lacquered ground. The central portion is hinged and opens to reveal a mirror with a chequer parquetry and inlaid interior. The frieze has ormolu panels depicting a winged sphinx flanked by foliate swags. This magnificent dressing table is a direct copy of the famous model by Adam Weisweiler (1744–1820), made in 1784 for Marie Antoinette who subsequently gave it to her confidante, Madame de Polignac. This table was rediscovered in a dealer's shop in 1840 and purchased by the Empress Eugénie in 1865. This copy was made by Alfred Beurdeley (1847–1919) who took over the family business in 1875 and specialized in the production of furniture of the most sumptuous quality.

Gaillard Dining Suite
c.1900

At A Glance

Date: c.1900
Origin: France
Brief description: A carved fruitwood dining suite designed by Eugène Gaillard.

The suite comprises a dining table and ten chairs with tolled leather upholstery, designed by Eugène Gaillard (1862–1933) and first exhibited at the Exposition Universelle, Paris, in 1900. Gaillard specialized in bedroom and dining room furniture and fittings, ranging from large sideboards and cupboards to small side-chairs and tables, distinguished by their rhythmic curvilinear character, both in form and decoration. This suite is very similar to that exhibited by Samuel Bing's Pavillon de l'Art Nouveau at the Exposition.

Vallin Dining Suite
1903

At A Glance

Date: 1903
Origin: France
Brief description: A carved
  walnut dining suite.

The suite comprises a dining table, 11 chairs, two sideboards, and a cabinet. It was commissioned in 1902 by the Dutreux family, who occupied the Château de la Celle-Saint-Cloud from 1844 to 1951. It was executed the following year to designs by Eugène Vallin (1856–1922), an architect and designer of the Nancy School. As an architect, he was a pioneer of reinforced concrete, but as an interior designer his excellent graphic work was occasionally marred by a tendency toward heaviness. He rejected the ornate qualities of Majorelle and insisted that the only decoration necessary in furniture was that created by the interplay of the lines of the furniture itself.

Guimard Art Nouveau Coiffeuse
1912

At A Glance

Date: 1912
Origin: France
Brief description: A fine carved pearwood and metal coiffeuse designed by Hector Guimard.

This elegant dressing table in the best Art Nouveau style has a curved top, set above three very shallow drawers, and a long narrow central drawer flanked by two smaller projecting drawers, mounted on tapering legs. The mirror is angled and has small rounded side mirrors. This table was designed by Hector Guimard (1867–1942), an architect and furniture designer who was strongly influenced by Victor Horta in the use of plant forms as inspiration. Although his lasting monument consists of the Art Nouveau entrances to the stations of the Paris Metro (1899–1904), he produced some beautiful furniture, mainly in pearwood, from 1900 onward.

Dunand Tables
c.1925

At A Glance

Date: c.1925
Origin: France
Brief description: A nest
of three lacquered wood
and eggshell tables by
Jean Dunand.

The form of these tables is simplicity itself, with their severely simple shape and rounded corners. Instead, the surfaces have been exquisitely covered with a distinctive style of lacquer. These little tables were the creation of the Swiss-born furniture maker Jean Dunand who established his atelier in the rue Halle, Paris. Originally trained as a jeweler specializing in dinanderie (pieces in non-precious metals), he turned to lacquer shortly before World War I and perfected techniques which had a major impact on the Art Deco furniture of the interwar years.

Leleu Table
1933–35

At A Glance

Date: 1933–35
Origin: France
Brief description: A glass-topped, chrome-mounted table designed by Jules Leleu.

The circular glass top incorporates an ivorine plaque. The cylindrical stem terminates in three shaped chrome-mounted feet. It was designed by Jules Leleu who burst dramatically on the scene when he first exhibited his furniture at the Salon des Artistes-Décorateurs in 1922 under the trade name of Dominique Leleu. Less lavish than Ruhlmann but probably more successful commercially, Leleu ranked among the three or four top furniture designers of France in the 1920s and 1930s.

Olbrich Table
1905

At A Glance

Date: 1905
Origin: Germany
Brief description: An inlaid and ebonized maple and burrwood table designed by Joseph Maria Olbrich.

The oval top is inlaid with a geometrical design in various woods and mother-of-pearl, mounted on two large square legs and smaller supports with a shaped base. It was designed by Joseph Maria Olbrich (1867–1908) as part of a suite intended for the music salon at the Mathildenhöhe in Darmstadt, commissioned by Grand Duke Ernst Ludwig of Hesse. Although this was undeniably his most important commission, Olbrich also designed a great deal of other furniture as well as metalwork and jewelry.

Rietveld Lady's Writing Desk
1935–36

At A Glance

Date: 1935–36
Origin: Holland
Brief description: A red lacquered lady's writing desk designed by Gerrit Rietveld.

The rectangular writing surface is placed above a cupboard door and two drawers, with a black plinth. It was designed by Gerrit Rietveld (1888–1964), the outstanding Dutch designer of his generation, for the Smedes residence at Den Dolder. The height of the writing surface was adapted to the height of the window sills which enlarged the working space. All the furniture in this house was executed in black, yellow, and red.

Lannuier Card Table
c.1815

At A Glance

Date: c.1815
Origin: USA
Brief description: A classical mahogany parcel-gilt and brass-mounted card table designed by Charles Honoré Lannuier.

The rectangular hinged top has canted corners and brass-inlaid edges and is set above a conforming frame with a brass mount over carved dolphin supports backed by leaf-carved animal-paw feet. It was probably designed by Charles Honoré Lannuier (1779–1819), one of the many French craftsmen who fled the revolution and settled in America at the end of the 18th century. Foremost among them was Lannuier who arrived at New York in 1803. Having trained in Paris he was well versed in the new designs and decorative treatments of the Empire Style.

Rohlfs Library Table
1901

At A Glance

Date: 1901
Origin: USA
Brief description: A carved oak library table designed by Charles Rohlfs.

This is an early example of the unique ability of the designer Charles Rohlfs to move effortlessly between the Arts and Crafts Movement and Art Nouveau esthetics. The powerful and deceptively simple character of this massive table reveals a judicious marriage of different timbers, harmonious proportions, and decorative features. Intended as a partner's desk, it is a unique piece, though very much in the style associated with Rohlfs. Born in New York, the son of an emigrant German cabinetmaker, Rohlfs moved to Buffalo in 1885. Although he had ambitions to become an actor, it was the furniture he executed for his own home that brought him to the attention of a wider public and led to many special commissions. In 1898 he established a commercial workshop and thereafter his fame and success were assured.

Frank Lloyd Wright End Table
c.1955

At A Glance

Date: c.1955
Origin: USA
Brief description: A mahogany end table by Frank Lloyd Wright.

The severely simple design, relieved only by a discreet Greek key pattern border, was designed for Heritage Hendredon by Frank Lloyd Wright (1869–1959). It epitomizes his philosophy, expressed in his own words: "The most truly satisfactory apartments are those in which most or all of the furniture is built in as part of the original scheme considering the whole as an integral unit." He advised his contemporaries to "bring out the nature of the materials, let their nature intimately into your scheme. Strip the wood of varnish and let it alone… Use the soft, warm, optimistic tones of earth and autumn leaves." Oak and poplar were the timbers which he favored for his furniture, although his designs were regarded as revolutionary at the time and he often had difficulty in finding cabinetmakers who were prepared to interpret them.

Charles I Cupboard
c.1630

At a Glance

Date: c.1630
Origin: Wales
Brief description: A Charles I oak deuddarn press cupboard dated 1630, the backboards and projecting top of the lower section replaced.

The original upper section has a molded cornice above a carved frieze centered by the carved inscription of 1630 over two paneled doors carved with stylized foliate. The lower section has two paneled doors over one long door on bracket feet with the tag Kendall Milne & Co, Depository, Manchester. The linen press dates from the 17th century and alludes to the large shallow drawers or sliding shelves on which linen was stored. Pieces like this are undervalued on account of modern fitted bedrooms, which leave little or no room to spare.

George I Bachelor's Chest
c.1720

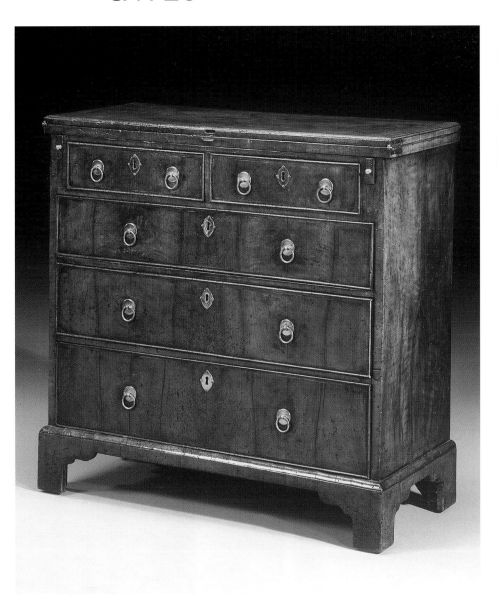

At a Glance

Date: c.1720
Origin: England
Brief description: A George I bachelor's chest in figured walnut.

This example is in figured walnut, which, together with the decorative flourishes, places it within the second decade of the 18th century. It is feather-banded overall, with a rectangular molded hinged crossbanded top, above two short and three long graduated drawers. Small chests such as this were designed to fit in the bedroom window pier. The term by which they are now known, however, did not come into use until the 19th century.

English Cupboard-on-chest
early 18th century

At a Glance

Date: Early 18th century
Origin: England
Brief description: An English oak cupboard-on-chest with molded cornice and panel door.

This piece of furniture represents an early attempt to save space by placing one form on top of another. It has a rather pleasing molded cornice and a twin-arched fielded panel door above a drawer, while the chest has two short and three long drawers, on stile feet.

Welsh Dresser
mid 18th century

At a Glance

Date: Mid 18th century
Origin: Wales
Brief description: An oak dresser from Conway Valley, North Wales.

The term Welsh dresser arose in the 19th century to describe a distinctive type of freestanding dresser, with a cupboard and drawers in the lower section and open shelves above. Despite the name, the majority of examples were produced in Lancashire and other parts of England, but in this particular case the epithet is apt, for it hails from the Conway Valley, North Wales. A peculiar characteristic of dressers from this area was that the plate racks contained small cupboards at their base. In this case the gap between the cupboards is filled with holly inlaid drawers and pierced fretwork, features which add considerably to its desirability.

George III Commode
1760–65

At a Glance

Date: 1760–65
Origin: England
Brief description: A George III ormolu-
mounted rosewood, fruitwood, and
marquetry bombé commode.

It is sumptuously veneered with parquetry and ormolu ornament. The serpentine fronted top is centered by a marquetry panel depicting a neoclassical urn profusely filled with blossom. The corners are inlaid with rose sprays while the molded cornice over the two long drawers is decorated with rosettes and cornucopias. It was executed in the early years of George III's reign by Pierre Langlois who flourished in London between 1759 and 1781 and had a high reputation for fine furniture in the style of Louis XV and Louis XVI, especially commodes such as this.

George III Bookcase
c.1780

At a Glance

Date: c.1780
Origin: England
Brief description: A George III mahogany secretaire breakfront bookcase.

The molded and dentilled cornice is centered by a serpentine arched pediment above a fluted and roundel frieze over two pairs of glazed doors with oval and shaped astragals. The base has a rosewood-banded secretaire drawer enclosing a fitted interior of drawers and pigeonholes, with a green baize-lined writing surface above a pair of paneled doors enclosing a shelf with four drawers on each side. This elegant bookcase has been attributed to the Golden Square firm of John Mayhew (d.1811) and William Ince (d.1804), a long-running partnership that received many major commissions from the English aristocracy. A brand mark on this bookcase reveals that it was once the property of the First Lord of the Treasury and Prime Minister in the reign of William IV (1830–37).

Welsh Cupboard
c.1800

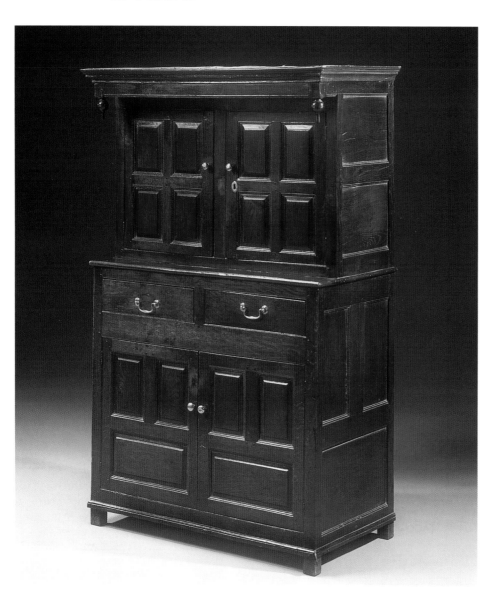

At a Glance

Date: c.1800
Origin: Wales
Brief description: A Welsh oak cupboard or Cwpwrdd deuddarn.

This example was probably made in Cardiganshire, to judge by its style. It has a moulded cornice and drop-pendant frieze above a pair of doors, each with four fielded panels. There are two frieze drawers and a pair of three-panel doors below, mounted on stile feet.

Regency Chest
c.1810

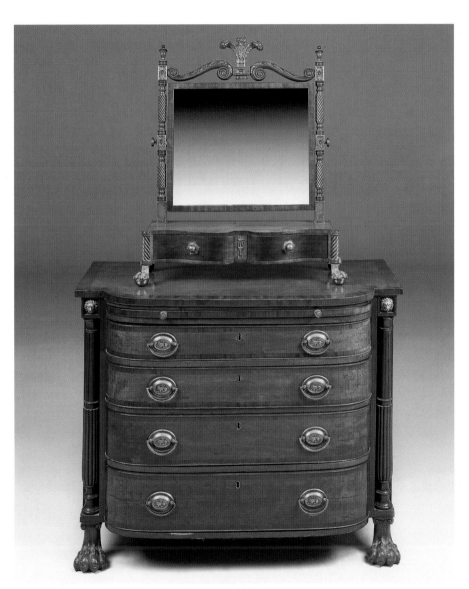

At a Glance

Date: c.1810
Origin: England
Brief description: A Regency mahogany and ebonized inlaid bowfront chest.

The crossbanded rectangular top is set above a green baize-lined slide and four part cedar-lined graduated drawers, flanked by a part-reeded baluster column headed by a lion mask. The bowfront shape of this chest is very similar to one published by Thomas Sheraton in the appendix to The Cabinet-Maker and Upholsterer's Drawing Book *of 1793.*

George III Bookcase
c.1780

The term breakfront denotes a piece of furniture where part of the front projects beyond the line of the rest, a style which applied to sideboards and wardrobes as well as bookcases. This example has a dentil-molded cornice with a swan's neck pediment that ends in rosettes above a pair of breakfronted glazed doors with arched mullions. The shelves are a later addition. The secretaire drawer opens to a fitted interior with pigeonholes and cedar-lined drawers above a pair of paneled doors.

Godwin Writing Desk
late 19th century

This desk, manufactured by William Watt for Dromore Castle in Ireland, was designed by Edward William Godwin, one of the foremost furniture designers in the second half of the 19th century and a major precursor of English Modernism. Above all, Godwin was strongly influenced by Japanese styles which had recently found their way to the western world. The rectangular top has three open recesses and three paneled slides above a fall-flap with hinged book-rest. The tooled leather, fitted interior is above a central cupboard flanked by short drawers.

Baillie Scott Sideboard
early 20th century

At a Glance

Date: Early 20th century
Origin: England
Brief description: An oak and inlaid sideboard attributed to Mackay Hugh Baillie Scott.

The raised back has a rectangular top above two open shelves, flanked by cupboard doors enclosing shelves decorated with inlaid daffodils. It is mounted on a breakfront base with two deep drawers and two cupboard doors, over an open shelf set on block feet. It is believed to have been designed by Mackay Hugh Baillie Scott (1865–1945). Despite his Scottish name, he was born in England and spent much of his career in the Isle of Man where several houses designed by him are still to be seen. Like his contemporary Mackintosh, he was an architect who attained a high international reputation, also producing furniture and metalwork strongly influenced by the Arts and Crafts Movement.

Liberty & Co. Sideboard
early 20th century

At A Glance

Date: Early 20th century
Origin: England
Brief description: A stained oak sideboard produced by Liberty & Co., London.

This rather somber piece is strongly redolent of the Middle Ages, and reflects the passion for the Gothic in much of the furniture produced by Liberty, the famous London store which had such a marked effect on Continental taste at the turn of the last century that lo Stile Liberty was the Italian name for Art Nouveau. The rectangular top is placed above a central cupboard door with dark-green bottle glass, flanked by open compartments, mounted on a cupboard with sloping sides on plain feet. The firm was founded by Sir Arthur Lasenby Liberty (1843–1917), the son of a Nottinghamshire lace manufacturer who established his famous Regent Street store in 1875.

Louis XIV Bureau Mazarin
c.1685

At A Glance

Date: c.1685
Origin: France
Brief description: A Louis XIV bureau mazarin attributed to Aubertin Gaudron.

This style of flat-topped bureau derives its name from Cardinal Mazarin (1602–61), the Italian-born cleric and diplomat who rose to become chief minister of France in 1642 and was also a leading patron of the arts. This fine example has a rectangular top, three drawers on either side, and square tapering legs, but it is lavishly decorated in amaranth, ebony, floral marquetry, and parcel-gilt ornament. It has been attributed to Aubertin Gaudron who supplied a great deal of fine pieces to the Garde-Meuble Royal between 1686 and 1713.

Louis XIV Bureau-plat
c.1700

At A Glance

Date: c.1700
Origin: France
Brief description: A Louis XIV ormolu-mounted, bureau-plat attributed to André-Charles Boulle.

This is the French term for a flat-topped writing desk with a frieze containing drawers. This splendid early example is decorated overall in contre-partie, the rounded rectangular overhanging top having tooled and gilt leather inset. It is lavishly ornamented with ormolu mounts, ebonized wood inlaid with tortoiseshell and brass-inlaid boulle marquetry, a veritable tour de force which has been identified as the work of André-Charles Boulle (1642–1732), the great maître-ébeniste who dominated French cabinetmaking in the long reign of Louis XIV and after whom this marquetry technique is named.

Van Risen Burgh *Bureau de Dame*
c.1730

At A Glance

Date: c.1730
Origin: France
Brief description: A Louis XV ormolu-mounted marquetry *bureau de dame* made by Bernard II van Risen Burgh (BRVB).

As the French term suggests, this small bureau was designed for ladies, and generally lighter in construction than the usual bureaus. This example has a concave-sided rectangular top with a molded border. The hinged flap is inlaid with a cartouche framed by C scrolls, opening to reveal a gilt-tooled green leather writing surface. The undulating sides and back have shaped panels decorated with trailing foliage. It was made by Bernard II van Risen Burgh (popularly known as BRVB), who flourished in Paris in the early part of the 18th century and was arguably the most famous cabinetmaker of the reign of Louis XV.

Napoleon III *Presentoir*

c.1855

At A Glance

Date: c.1855
Origin: France
Brief description: A Napoleon III bronze-mounted oak and ebony *presentoir* by Alexandre-Georges Fourdinois.

This French term denotes an ornate piece of furniture which was designed to show off the choicest objects of vertu. This extraordinary example is surmounted by a stepped pediment, with a riot of baluster finials, gadrooned frieze, and pierced foliate galleries. The breakfront platform is above two cupboard doors flanked by paneled doors with stylized foliate hinges . It was made by Alexandre-Georges Fourdinois (1799–1871) who established his atelier in 1835 and became one of the leading cabinetmakers of the Second Empire. At the Paris Exposition of 1855 he received the medaille d'honneur, the highest award, and was appointed an officer of the Legion d'Honneur seven years later. His clients included members of the Imperial family and the aristocracy.

Giroux *Bombé Bureau de Dame* c.1860

At A Glance

Date: c.1860
Origin: France
Brief description: A Napoleon III *bombé bureau de dame* made by Alphonse-Gustave Giroux, Paris.

The term bombé *(literally "bulging")* describes the swelling shape of chests of drawers and commodes fashionable in the reign of Louis XIV and invariably decorated in the Rococo style. This lady's bureau reflects the passion for the styles of the early 18th century which were revived so enthusiastically in the Second Empire period. This bureau is notable for the Maltese cross motifs applied overall in pewter and the delicate blend of walnut, tulipwood, and ebonized timbers. It was made by Alphonse-Gustave Giroux at Paris.

Napoleon III Side Cabinet
c.1865

At A Glance

Date: c.1865
Origin: France
Brief description: A Napoleon III ormolu-mounted mahogany and marquetry side cabinet.

Surmounted by a white marble top, it has a pierced gallery rail above a long shallow drawer. The twin cupboard doors are exquisitely decorated with ormolu, each centered by two interlaced Ls and a fleur de lis surmounted by a royal coronet. This cabinet was made by Guillaume-Edmond Lexcellent who sprang to prominence with his striking designs exhibited at the Paris Exposition of 1867. He continued to be known as a manufacturer of high-quality (if rather expensive) furniture until well into the 20th century.

Diehl Side Cabinet
c.1870

At A Glance

Date: c.1870
Origin: France
Brief description: A Napoleon III side cabinet attributed to Charles-Guillaume Diehl.

This cabinet has been richly ornamented with ormolu-mounted porcelain panels contrasting with ebony and ebonized woods. The shaped top is of grey marble within an egg and dart overhanging rim and the frieze is decorated with a scrolling cartouche featuring a classical female figure flanked by foliate branches. The plaques on the cupboard doors depict landscapes and lake scenes. The sides of the cabinet are decorated with gilt lions' masks above scrolling foliate and lambrequin terminals. This extravaganza has all the hallmarks of Charles-Guillaume Diehl who took the Exposition Universelle of 1867 by storm with his luxuriously eclectic pieces whose ornament was derived from Greek, Etruscan, Egyptian, Gothic, and Oriental forms.

Durand Bookcases

c.1880

At A Glance

Date: c.1880
Origin: France
Brief description: A pair of ormolu-mounted kingwood open bookcases.

Each is headed by a shaped marble top, above three adjustable shelves flanked by a foliate scallop clasp. The apron is centered by a scrolling foliate swag and each bookcase stands on four scroll feet with foliate sabots. Both bookcases are liberally stamped "G. Durand." Gervais Durand was the son of a cabinetmaker who operated from various workshops in Paris in the latter part of the 19th century and was joined by his son Frédéric-Louis about 1890 when the firm changed its name to Durand et Fils.

Dubois *Bonheur-du-jour*
c.1920

At A Glance

Date: c.1920
Origin: France
Brief description: An ormolu-mounted *bonheur-du-jour* made by A. Dubois.

This French term (literally "happiness of the day") signifies a lady's writing desk, distinguished by its elaborately fitted accessories. This example is in rosewood and kingwood decorated with green-stained marquetry in motifs of cups and flower-filled vases. It is surmounted by a three-quarter pierced gallery above a marble top. The front has two sliding barrel panels opening to reveal a large pigeonhole above three small drawers with a secret drawer to the right side. It is supported on four cabriole legs, each headed by a grotesque mask. It was made by the sculptor and cabinetmaker, A. Dubois in the manner of Charles Topino.

Ruhlmann Bookcase
c.1925

At A Glance

Date: c.1925
Origin: France
Brief description: A Macassar ebony bookcase.

This striking example has open and compartmented shelves raised on a contemporary black painted rectangular plinth. It bears the B in a circle mark of Emile-Jacques Ruhlmann (1879–1933) and marks the transition from his earlier neoclassical work to furniture more strongly influenced by Cubism.

Olbrich Vitrine
1905

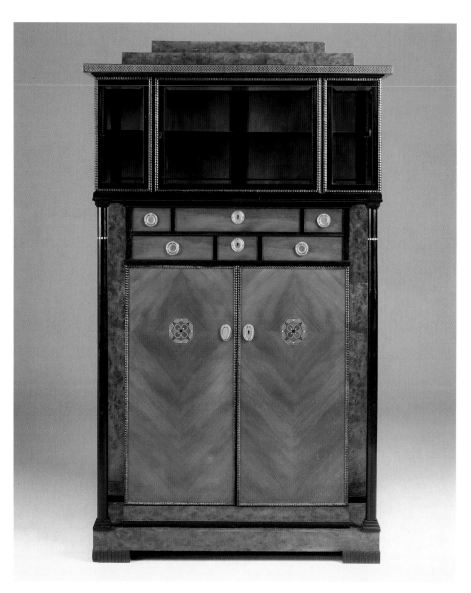

At A Glance

Date: 1905
Origin: Germany
Brief description: An inlaid and ebonized maple and burrwood vitrine by Joseph Maria Olbrich.

This exquisite cabinet is finely inlaid with mother-of-pearl and banded with ebonized reeding and fitted with gilt handles and lockplate. It was designed for the music salon at the Mathildenhöhe artists' colony in Darmstadt by Joseph Maria Olbrich and it is interesting to compare it with the cabinet designed by Moser, previously noted. A similar example may be seen at the Bröhan Museum in Berlin.

Hoffmann Bookcase

early 20th century

At A Glance

Date: Early 20th century
Origin: Austria
Brief description: An oak and
ebonized wood bookcase
attributed to Josef Hoffmann.

*The rectangular superstructure
has three glazed doors recessed
within a ribbed rounder rectangular frame while the serpentine
plinth base encloses two fluted
drawers with circular pad handles. The design is attributed to
Josef Hoffmann (1870–1955), the
Austrian architect, graphic artist,
and designer who became one
of the leading figures of the
Vienna Sezession at the turn of
the last century.*

Winchester Sideboard
c.1802

At A Glance

Date: c.1802
Origin: USA
Brief description: A Federal inlaid cherrywood sideboard designed by William Winchester.

The rectangular top has a serpentine front above a conforming case with a string-inlaid long drawer over a pair of cupboard doors, and mounted on tapering legs with banded cuffs. It was commissioned by General James Winchester (1752–1826) of Maryland and Tennessee at the beginning of the 19th century when he and his wife Susan were furnishing their new house. It was actually designed and constructed by the general's nephew William Winchester (b.1781), a cabinetmaker from his home state of Maryland. The appellation "Federal" alludes to the period in American politics when the Federalist party was in the ascendant, and thus it signifies an epoch, just as Regency or Louis XVI are used in Britain and France.

Federal Secretary Bookcase
c.1820

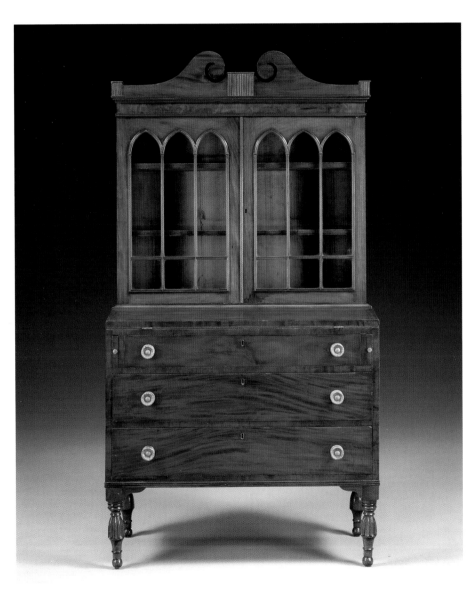

At A Glance

Date: c.1820
Origin: USA
Brief description: A Federal mahogany secretary bookcase made by Joseph Short, from Massachusetts.

Although the term "secretary" or "secretaire" was originally applied to a piece of furniture designed specifically for writing, it began to acquire a more general meaning after Thomas Sheraton merely stated that it defined any "pieces of furniture to write at." This particular piece is in two distinct parts. The upper portion is a glass-fronted bookcase, fitted to a case with a hinged writing flap over three graduated long drawers, mounted on ring-turned and tapering lotus carved feet. The brass handles appear to be original. It is believed to have been constructed by Joseph Short (1771–1819) of Newburyport, Massachusetts.

Greene & Greene Sideboard
1907

At A Glance

Date: 1907
Origin: USA
Brief description: A redwood sideboard designed by Charles and Henry Greene for the Lon Franklin Chapin House, Pasadena, California.

Four central drawers are flanked by cabinets opening to reveal two shelves and there is a single wooden back rail. This sturdy sideboard is of pegged construction with brass nail ornament. It was designed by Charles and Henry Greene for the Lon Franklin Chapin House, Pasadena, California. No less an authority than Charles Robert Ashbee wrote of Charles Greene's work that it was "among the best there is in this country… Like Lloyd Wright, the spell of Japan is upon him, like Lloyd Wright he feels the beauty and makes magic out of the horizontal line, but there is more tenderness, more subtlety, more self-effacement…"

George II Wine Cooler
c.1740

At a Glance

Date: c.1740
Origin: England
Brief description: A George II mahogany wine cooler.

The taste for white wines which developed in the first half of the 18th century led to the demand for vessels designed to chill them, hence the wine cooler which was designed to hold a bottle packed with ice. The earliest examples were made in ceramics or glass and later in silver or electroplate, but larger examples, capable of holding several bottles, were generally made of wood with a glass or ceramic lining. This example has an oval brass-bound body. The brass liner was designed to hold bottles of wine in ice.

George II Washstand
c.1750

At a Glance

Date: c.1750
Origin: England
Brief description: A George II
mahogany corner washstand.

This attractive little piece is inlaid overall with boxwood lines and crossbanded in tulipwood. The arched gallery has a small shelf above a bow-fronted top with circular holes for the washing bowl, while the central tier has a drawer flanked by simulated drawers on square layered legs joined by a stretcher with a central molded circle. Thomas Sheraton illustrates just such a washstand in the appendix to The Cabinet-Maker and Upholster's Drawing Book, reissued in London in 1802.

George II Candle Stands
c.1750

At a Glance

Date: c.1750
Origin: England
Brief description: A matched pair of George II candle stands in mahogany with parcel-gilt ornament.

Sometimes known by the French term of torchère, *these portable stands were the forerunner of the standard lamp of a later era. The earliest forms tended to be quite large and were designed to stand on a floor, but later examples were often smaller and intended to stand on top of a table or sideboard. This pair is in mahogany with parcel-gilt ornament. Each has a circular tray-top edged with egg-and-dart ornament. The partly turned and tapering octagonal shaft with central foliate band is mounted on a tripod base ending in pad feet. Small pieces of furniture like this have proved a good investment.*

George III Bedside Cupboard
late 18th century

The three-quarter galleried top has a hinged and upward-folding paneled shutter while the cabinet is mounted on tapering paneled legs and gadrooned knob feet. Though no piece of this exact pattern is known by Thomas Chippendale (1718–79), all of its features are found in well-attested examples of his work.

Regency Quartetto Tables
c.1810

At a Glance

Date: c.1810
Origin: England
Brief description: A set of Regency rosewood quartetto tables of a similar design to one published by Thomas Sheraton.

This term is given to nests of four small tables in descending order of size, designed to fit inside each other when not in use and thus saving space. This set is distinguished by crossbanding in padouk and satinwood. Each table has a rounded rectangular top above two turned tapering trestle-end column supports, joined by a bowed stretcher, on tapering splayed feet. This nest of tables is very similar to a design published in 1803 by Thomas Sheraton (1751–1806).

Dresser Umbrella Stand
late 1880s

At a Glance

Date: Late 1880s
Origin: England
Brief description: A Coalbrookdale cast-iron umbrella stand. Designed by Christopher Dresser.

It was designed by Christopher Dresser (1834–1904) and belongs to the period in the 1880s when he organized the somewhat ephemeral Art Furniture Alliance which produced furniture and metalwork combining Gothic and Japanese art forms. The pierced rectangular back is cast in the form of a Gothic arch, with scrolling tendrils and a geometric motif. The umbrella rest has brackets above a detachable trough. Coalbrookdale, famed for its iron foundries, was in the forefront of the Industrial Revolution from 1760 onward.

Watt Corner Cupboard
late 19th century

At a Glance

Date: Late 19th century
Origin: England
Brief description: An important pine corner cupboard made by William Watt for Dromore Castle, Ireland.

Like the writing desk previously noted, this corner cupboard was manufactured by William Watt for Dromore Castle, Ireland, to a design by Edward W. Godwin. The paneled back has a triangular pediment inset with raffia panels, while the canted base has a marble top, above a single paneled cupboard door flanked by open recesses.

Gimson Cabinet

c.1920

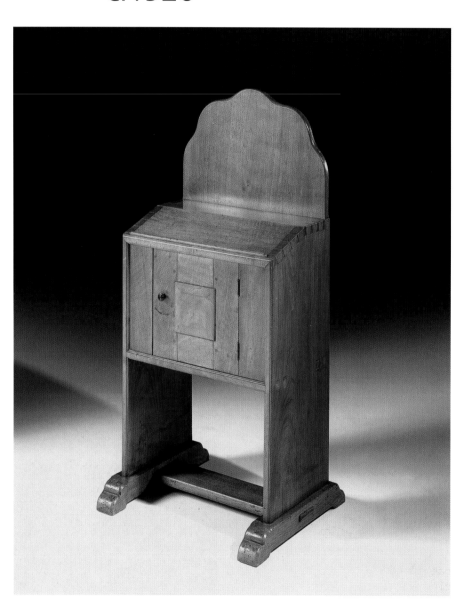

At a Glance

Date: c.1920
Origin: England
Brief description: A small
    walnut cabinet.

The undulating back panel supports a single door compartment with central raised square panels, fitted with a circular ebony lockplate, the whole mounted on stepped bracket feet. It was produced by Ernest Gimson (1864–1919), one of the foremost artist-craftsmen of the early 20th century and a worthy successor to William Morris. He was closely associated with the Arts and Crafts Movement before establishing the Cotswold School of cabinetmakers who included Sidney and Ernest Barnsley.

Russell Chest of Drawers and Sideboard
c.1930

Sir Gordon Russell (1892–1980) established a family furniture business in the Cotswold village of Broadway where fine quality handmade and machine-made furniture is produced to this day. Individual pieces, dating from the 1920s, were based on designs by the Finnish architect Alvar Aalto and the Thonet brothers. He also produced his own highly distinctive style, exemplifed in this satin birch dwarf chest of drawers with dove tailing and pegging and oak sideboard with overhanging molded top above a short frieze drawer.

At a Glance

Date: c.1930
Origin: England
Brief description: A satin birch dwarf chest of drawers and oak sideboard by Gordon Russell.

Barbedienne *Guéridon*

c.1880

At a Glance

Date: c.1880
Origin: France
Brief description: A gilt-bronze and malachite *guéridon* by Ferdinand Barbedienne.

This French term denotes an ornamental stand designed to hold a candelabrum or torch, although latterly used to house a basket or drinks tray. They came into fashion in the reign of Louis XV but were revived during the Second Empire and remained popular till the end of the 19th century. The earliest examples had the top supported by gilt and ebony figures of blackamoors, but later they were superseded by female allegorical figures as in this case. Both the circular top and the triform base are in malachite, the cast-bronze figures being richly gilded. It bears the mark of the well-known bronze founder Ferdinand Barbedienne.

Louis XV-style *Secretaire à Abattant*
1883

At A Glance

Date: 1883
Origin: France
Brief description: A Louis XV-style, ormolu-mounted, mahogany, and lacquered *secretaire à abattant*.

This is a rather fancy term for a writing cabinet fitted with flaps. In this instance it has a shaped spreading pediment inset with a conforming frieze drawer above a waisted case with veneered sides. The front is decorated with a wavy panel depicting cranes flying over a hilly landscape. This particular example is a copy of a celebrated original by Jean-François Dubut of Paris about 1760, and was made by Henri Dasson (d.1896) whose atelier at 106 rue Vieille du Temple specialized in fine reproductions of pieces from the reigns of Louis XIV to Louis XVI.

Gallé Dragonfly Table

c.1900

This exquisite little table in the finest Art Nouveau tradition was designed by Emile Gallé (1846–1904) the leader of the Nancy School. Although best known for the jewelry and glass which dominated his career, from 1885 onward he also designed and produced furniture, resolutely ignoring the eclecticism of so many of his contemporaries and concentrating entirely on natural forms. His furniture had suitably exotic names, such as Heureux les Pacifiques (blessed are the peacemakers), Les Parfums d'Autrefois (bygone fragrances) or, more prosaically, Aux Feuilles de Bananier (with banana leaves). He also specialized in meubles parlants (speaking furniture) which incorporated lines of poetry worked in marquetry.

Majorelle Marquetry Table
c.1900

At A Glance

Date: c.1900
Origin: France
Brief description: An ormolu-mounted, marquetry table designed by Louis Majorelle.

This tiny table has three shallow drawers with side flaps, mounted on slender, tapering legs and gilt feet. It was designed by Louis Majorelle (1859–1929) who came under the influence of Gallé, but also brought a distinctive sculptural technique to bear on the furniture he designed from 1890 onward. Majorelle himself counselled, "The first need in the construction of a piece of furniture is to seek a healthy structure capable of inspiring a sense of harmony and such that the essential lines should have an architectural sense of elegant proportion."

Vallin Pedestal
c.1900

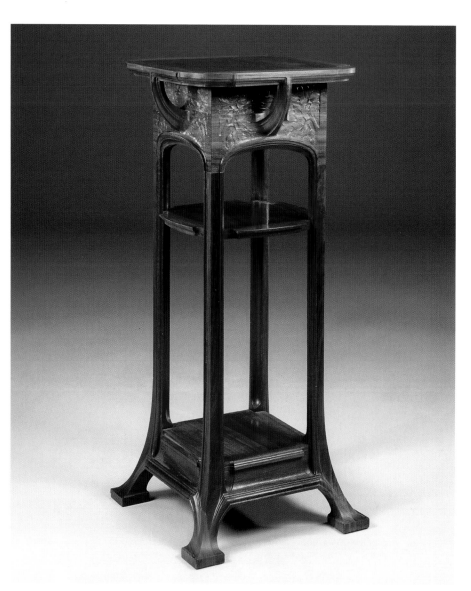

At A Glance

Date: c.1900
Origin: France
Brief description: A carved
  pedestal by Eugène Vallin.

The three-tiered pedestal is finely carved and decorated with plane leaves and fruits and bears the carved cypher EVALN of the artist-craftsman, Eugène Vallin (1856–1922), another of the Nancy School who were tremendously influenced by Gallé. Although he designed a wide range of furniture, Vallin is now regarded at his best in his small pieces, like pedestals and tripods, which have seldom been surpassed for elegance and lightness, features that were not always apparent in his larger pieces.

Art Nouveau Vitrine
c.1900

At A Glance

Date: c.1900
Origin: France
Brief description: An Art Nouveau mahogany vitrine in the style of Victor Horta.

Small cabinets of this kind with glazed doors were designed to display tiny objects of vertu. This particular example has a rectangular tiled top with a sinuous carved surround, above an open recess and glazed cupboard door. There are small projecting side shelves with carved brackets and the whole is mounted on shaped legs. It is in the style of Victor Horta (1861–1947), a Belgian architect and designer who, from 1892, turned his back on rigid classicism and developed a highly individualistic style which has been described as a tangle of writhing curves. He himself confessed (1895), "I abandoned the flower and leaf and turned instead to the stalk."

Gray Screen

c.1923

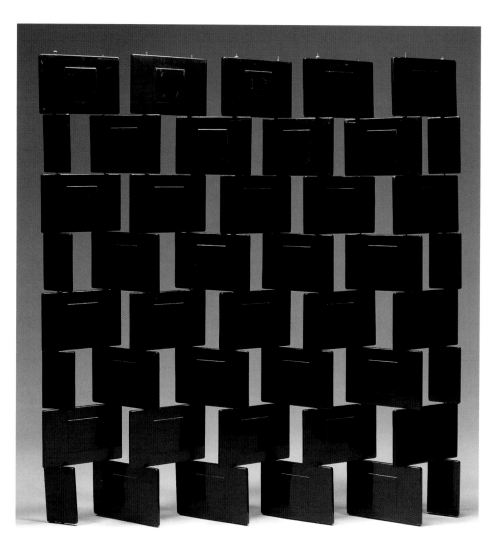

Having learned the technique of lacquering from Mr Charles of London and subsequently studied under the Japanese master Sugawara in Paris, Eileen Gray (1878–1976) applied it to furniture, wall paneling, and screens. Her first commission came after she exhibited her lacquerware at the 1913 Salon des Artistes Décorateurs and came to the attention of the leading coutourier Jacques Doucet. This led to the development of more abstract work of which this screen is a typical example, the blocks being lacquered in contrasting colors or black and white. This particular screen was originally the property of Jean Badovici, Gray's longtime friend and collaborator.

Albers Occasional Table

c.1933

At A Glance

Date: c.1933
Origin: Germany
Brief description: A steel and rosewood occasional table designed by Josef Albers and presented to Wassily Kandinsky.

The circular top has a surface of rectangular marquetry and is mounted on nickel-plated tubular uprights extending to form stretchers. It was designed by one artist-craftsman for another, reflecting the symbiosis between the fine arts and the applied arts in the interwar period. Josef Albers (1888–1976), the painter, designer, and head of the furniture workshop at the Dessau Bauhaus, presented it to his close friend, the Russian born painter Wassily Kandinsky (1866–1944), who had been the head of the Bauhaus at Weimar. The table may have been handed over shortly before both Albers and Kandinsky fled Nazi Germany, the one to settle in the USA and the other to move to France.

Paint-decorated Blanket Chest
1807

At A Glance

Date: 1807
Origin: USA
Brief description: A paint-decorated blanket chest with the inscription "MAL OWER 1807."

The rectangular applied molded top has paint-decorated oval reserves at either end, above a conforming case fitted with a till and secret drawer. The central astragal panel is decorated with tulips and rosettes, as well as squiggle motifs surrounding the inscription "MAL OWER 1807" which not only pinpoints the date of manufacture but suggests an origin in Dauphin County, Southeast Pennsylvania, borne out by the fact that it alluded to Mary Over who married Henry Rife in 1827. The chest remained in the possession of the Rife (Reiff) family of Mennonites for many generations.

Stickley Bridal Chest
c.1902

Plain, solid, no-nonsense furniture, mostly executed in oak, was very much the hallmark of Gustav Stickley (1857–1942) who made this little chest bound by wrought iron hasps and brackets at the beginning of the 20th century. Stickley expressed his philosophy in October 1901, saying that he proposed "to substitute the luxury of taste for the luxury of costliness; to teach that beauty does not imply elaboration or ornament; to employ only those forms and materials which make for simplicity, individuality and dignity of effect."

At A Glance

Date: c.1902
Origin: USA
Brief description: An oak bridal chest by Gustav Stickley.

Eames Child's Stool

c.1945

At A Glance

Date: c.1945
Origin: USA
Brief description: A molded birch plywood child's stool by Charles and Ray Eames.

Charles and Ray Eames designed several furniture models for children around 1945, including tables, chairs, and stools. The latter exhibit a compound curve molding into the legs which served to add strength and support. They were launched at a press preview in New York that year and were critically acclaimed by the Museum of Modern Art, but they failed to catch on with the public. Although offered at various stores for a time, production ceased in 1947.

Frank Lloyd Wright Accessory Tables
c.1955

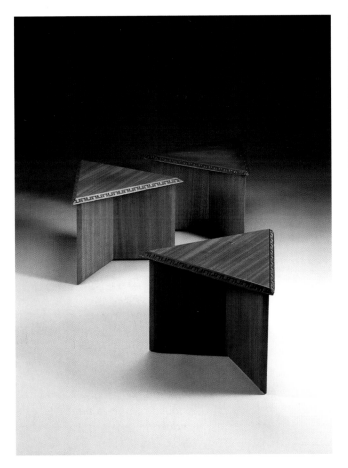

This intriguing suite was designed for Heritage Hendredon by Frank Lloyd Wright (1869–1959). Although oak and poplar were the timbers which he favored most for his furniture, he occasionally explored the potential of other woods, such as the hardwood mahogany. Initially he preferred handmade furniture. Echoing the tenets of the English Arts and Crafts Movement, but later he came to appreciate the qualities which could be attained by mechanical processes, to which he referred as, "the clean cut, straight-line forms that the machine can render far better than would be possible by hand."